ISLAND YEAR

Drawings by LAURIE OLIN

University of Washington Press

SEATTLE AND LONDON

ISLAND YEAR

by Hazel Heckman

Copyright © 1972 by the University of Washington Press
Printed in the United States of America

Library of Congress Cataloging in Publication Data

Heckman, Hazel.
  Island year.

  Bibliography: p.
  1. Natural history—Washington (State)—Anderson island.
I. Title.
QH105.W2H4   500.9'797'78   74–178701
ISBN 0–295–95171–0

For EARLE

One generation passeth away, and another generation cometh; but the earth abideth forever.

ECCLESIASTES 1:4

PREFACE

I suppose it may seem presumptuous to launch yet another book about an area so small and so circumscribed as Anderson Island. On the other hand, the two previous Island books (*Island Memoir* by Betsey Johnson Cammon and my own *Island in the Sound*) dealt primarily with the human population, past and present. This one pertains principally to the ecological world of nature, without which the Island would be a barren waste, unfit for *any* habitation.

I think it was a dead bird that prompted or persuaded me to start an annual record of fauna and flora observed on Anderson Island. Because of mainland commitments, my husband and I were still week-enders here. (Now, as native Vermonters say of relative newcomers, we are "permanent summer people.") During the five weekdays in winter immediately prior to our moving here as year-around residents, we occupied the upper floor of a split-level house in Tacoma, perched on a wooded hillside that sloped down to salt water. From the front deck of this apartment we could see the Island slip, and see the ferry *Tahoma* set out and return, and watch a portion of the crossings.

The bird was a western tanager, scarlet and yellow and black, with white wing bars. Confused in flight by the reflection in the picture window that gave us a scenic view of Puget Sound water filtered between fir, madroña, and dogwood trees, the tanager struck the glass head on. Some-times such an accident only stuns. The victim lies as though dead for an hour or so, then regains his senses and takes flight. This one still lay on the deck the following morning, a silent rebuke, a bit of color lost to the world he had en-riched and decorated. For as long as we lived in the split level the fatal collisions continued. I found dead juncos, house and purple finches, rusty and white-crowned spar-rows, a cedar waxwing, a golden-crowned kinglet. Robins, seemingly more expendable because of numbers, most often met disaster.

Following the publication of *Island in the Sound,* which contained casual references to wildlife protection, I began to receive uneasy letters. An eastern woman wrote that she had walked in the woods following an aerial spray for Dutch elm disease and had seen no rabbits or squirrels and only a few birds, where all had been abundant. A west-erner reported an unexplained dearth of jackrabbits. Letters came from here and there about polluted water, dead fish, the disappearance of coyotes and of golden eagles. One con-cerned reader, George Munford, of Grayling, Michigan, sent a year's membership to *Defenders of Wildlife.*

During the three-year period from January 1966 through December 1968 I kept a daily record of fauna and flora ob-served during walks on the Island. The entries for given dates each successive year show a remarkable similarity. Two years out of three I saw the first violet-green swallow on the same day. In the third book the event was re-corded only forty-eight hours later. Dates varied little for the first wood lily seen, the first trillium. In an era of unrest I found a certain blind assurance in this dependable rhythm of natural succession. The junco came in October and took his leave in April. Even "happenings" had their appointed time. The ebb and flow of the tides upon which so many lives depended were as faithful as was the rising and setting of the sun, the phasing of the moon, the appearance of the planets and the constellations, the periodic meteor showers, the orbit and the turning of the earth on its axis.

I found, oddly enough considering the small space it occupies, that the Island could be sectioned into climatic and geographic zones for exploration. On any given day a variation in temperature of several degrees might occur between sections only a mile or two apart. In some areas jackpines crowded firs and cedars along the fringes of the woods; in others, trees commonly known as white oak grew in profusion. Service, ninebark, and mountain balm had their favorite niches.

With so much to be seen, so much to be brought home for identification as to species, I made slow progress. The Island came to seem much larger than was actually the case. Some areas I visited again and again, having seen in dormancy what I wanted to see in leaf, in bloom, in fruit. I tried to catch the first emergence of red-flower currant, oso-berry, and skunk cabbage, to follow the slow shading of wake robin from clear white to rich rose-purple before the petals dropped.

Woods in places were so deep and dense, so nearly impenetrable as to be invested with mystery. One could see no more than ten feet beyond the fence row that defined the roadway. Lost once in our own back acre, I circled for thirty minutes without any sense of direction. I explored woods where only an occasional ray of sunlight penetrated. From a thick carpet of conifer needles came saprophytes of ethereal beauty—coral mushrooms, orange jelly cups, once an unexpected patch of golden chanterelles—and miniature deer, sword, and lady ferns, a sudden spread of perfoliate miner's lettuce, a rare greenish orchid called rattlesnake plantain.

After two or three years of exploration (often trespassing, for which I publicly apologize), I felt that the Island was as comfortable, as familiar, as an old worn shoe. To find myself alone in a wood or on an empty road lent a feeling of undiluted serenity.

The listing of fauna and flora in this book makes no pretense of being exhaustive. Nor is the text meant to be any kind of field guide. I explore and identify solely to satisfy my own curiosity, and for pleasure. Many good books, of which I have made wide use, are available. Nor is this treatise meant to be a swan song for the Island as I have known it. Despite saw, ax, dynamite, earth-mover, and ambitious man, the larger portion of the land mass remains essentially unblemished.

Although the contents of this book are based primarily on my own observations of fauna and flora during some twenty years of wandering about the Island, and I am solely responsible for any errors in identification of species, I am indebted to a great number of authors and trained experts in the field of nature.

I would like especially to mention the late E. A. Kitchin. From his own familiarity with Anderson Island birds, Mr. Kitchin marked for me his *Distributional Check-list of the Birds of the State of Washington*. Other particularly helpful books are C. P. Lyons' *Trees, Shrubs and Flowers to Know in Washington,* Stanley Jewett *et al., Birds of Washington State,* Erna Gunther's *Ethnobotany of Western Washington,* and Roger Tory Peterson's *Field Guide to Western Birds,* as well as Dr. Dixy Lee Ray's telecasts from the Pacific Science Center. I was further assisted by all of the books and publications mentioned in the bibliography.

I am grateful to any number of people who offered encouragement and help in this project. I would like to thank Murray Morgan for reading the manuscript and for his suggestions following the first draft of the book; Dorothy Barnard, who helped me with the mechanics; Islanders Billy and Harold Hansen, for their accounts and records of plants and birds observed; and Sam Tokarczyk, for his information concerning Island mushrooms. I am especially indebted to Jane Cammon, Island librarian, for her helpfulness in obtaining books requested, and to the personnel of Pierce County Library headquarters for their cooperation in the matter of seeking these out.

I would like to express appreciation to my husband Earle for his patience, his interest, and his help during the years of wandering and gathering information, to my son Jim and his wife Liane, and to my granddaughters Hollie and Lael for keeping me company during woods and beach excursions and calling my attention to that which I might otherwise have missed.

HAZEL HECKMAN

Anderson Island, Washington
March 1971

CONTENTS

ISLAND YEAR

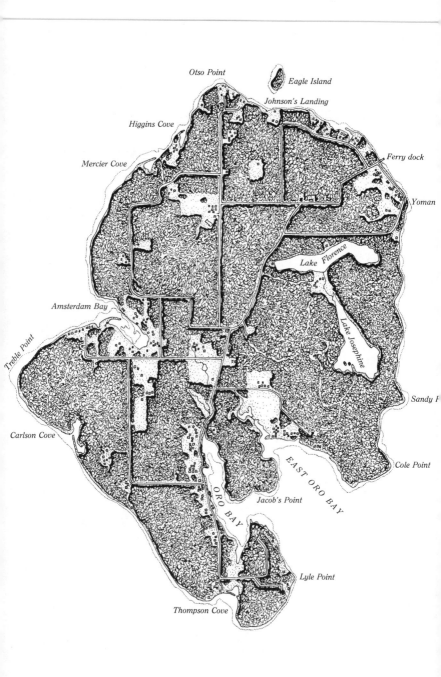

Otso Point

Eagle Island

Johnson's Landing

Higgins Cove

Ferry dock

Mercier Cove

Yoman

Lake Florence

Amsterdam Bay

Lake Josephine

Treble Point

Sandy P

Carlson Cove

Cole Point

EAST ORO BAY

Jacob's Point

ORO BAY

Lyle Point

Thompson Cove

INTRODUCTION

Seen from the air, the (approximately) six-by-three-mile chunk of real estate known as Anderson Island resembles a wooded oasis surrounded by water. To the east, in Carr Inlet, lie Fox Island, the shoe-shaped bulk of McNeil, the small islands, Ketron and Eagle. Nisqually Reach stretches to the south and west. On the north the waters of Balch Passage run fast during incoming and outgoing tides in their haste to crowd through The Narrows between Gig Harbor and wooded Point Defiance of the city of Tacoma.

Served by the ferry *Islander* from Steilacoom, the oldest incorporated town in the state of Washington, Anderson boasts a small, slightly fluctuating, year-around rural population. The Island's fourteen miles of shore line, cut by coves and inlets, are mostly high bank. Along the sloping sides of the several gulches, springs arise at intervals to replenish the crystal-clear, fresh-water streams, bordered by ferns and other growth, that terminate in estuaries on the graveled beaches. Nine sections of land, still largely uncleared, support a wealth of varied flora, much of it evergreen, and a thriving colony of wildlife.

Terrain rises from sea level to approximately four hundred feet. On the higher portion, two fresh-water lakes, Florence and Josephine, are fed by underwater springs. A section of swamp and bog runs through the center of the Island. At the

3

head of Oro Bay, in the southern half, lies a salt-tolerant marshland. It would be difficult to find or to imagine an area more diverse for biological exploration, a community where plant, animal, and man enjoy a closer interrelationship.

January

Broadleaf Evergreens

In lower Puget Sound country, protected on the north and west by the Olympic Mountain Range and to the east by the high Cascades, spring begins in January. We may have snow. During a quarter of a century of Januaries here we have experienced a half-dozen snows. A few of these, I suppose, might be described as "blizzards" by the uninitiated. But underneath the white, the growth remains emerald

5

green. Given a day of thaw, frozen leaves rise with restored color. Green boughs shake off their burden. Pussy willows proceed to open buds along the roadside. On more than one New Year's Day we have mowed the lawn and brought a rose inside.

To a plainswoman, broadleaf evergreens still seem something of a miracle. Prior to coming here, I was unaware of the term, or it had no meaning. Autumn, here as elsewhere, has always been my favorite season. Here, I like to see the bronzing of bracken in the fall, the shapes of bare trees silhouetted—boughs of broadleaf maple (not an evergreen), gnarled crowns of oak, groves of red alder persuaded in youth by prevailing winds and leaning one way, like old men carrying a burden of branches up a slope. I am stirred by *first* emergences, the radiance and tenderness of swollen buds and leaves like tiny wings unfolding. Green-all-winter seems an almost too kind favor.

Of ferns and fern allies along the roadsides, only bracken and its spore-producing distant relative, the common horsetail, a scouring rush, are missing in January, a month as green if not as flowering as any other. In January the earth shows promise but no anxiety. January, the month of Janus, the god of beginnings, is in no hurry. Even to the watchful and the wary, change comes slowly. By June you want to hold back growth, to watch a bud, a flower, a fruit develop. But January is a relaxed month, a deliberate month, a making ready.

In January, winter jasmine bloomed, canary-yellow, behind the patio and forsythia, brought inside, opened slowly in golden preview. Alder boughs burned a paced red against the ranked green of conifers, hills clothed with evergreens. Bare dogwood trees took on a rosy haze. Boles of young madroñas were smooth coral satin, unmarked by the chartreuse patches that would open later.

Precariously rooted along the high-bank east shore, madroñas leaned toward the gray water. Earth-softening rains took their toll: trees gave way, slid, stood on their heads, and came to rest finally across rocky beaches, red and green boughs laved by salt water. The bark was lovely to the touch. I thought of a letter from a woman in Nova Scotia who had spent her childhood on Puget Sound. "I read about Madroñas in your book," she wrote. As a child she had liked to lay her cheek against the bark. She had tried in vain to persuade the tree to grow in Nova Scotia.

Madroña is a tree of *western* North America, also spelled madroño and madrone. I have never heard a Canadian refer to it by other than its scientific name *arbutus*. Michael Luark, who logged on Anderson Island in 1854 and wrote about the tree in his diary with a kind of wonder, called it "laurel," which the leaf somewhat resembles. Wood is hard and burns slowly, leaving a fine ash. The tree lives for a long time. Ricked lengths make the woodpile so colorful that I consign them to the fire with reluctance.

Old, leathery leaves fall at intervals, as fresh green tufts appear, rattle and skip before a wind and decline to disintegrate. Burning, they give off a bitter odor. Gardeners say both leaves and ash of madroña poison soil. But "beauty is its own excuse for being," and this striking member of the heath family is spectacular in any size or season, the first tree a stranger asks to have identified. The thin rocky detritus of Island soil is especially to its liking. January woods, for all their greenery, would be drab and lifeless without the tree's bright presence.

No longer harassed by hunters, mallards and American widgeon gathered in Island coves and inlets to feed and gossip. When I walked down the trail to Higgins Cove, they spooked out slowly, thrashing water, assumed grace once airborne, and circled back to look me over. Even at ebb tide in January, the cove is a favorite feeding ground.

The brilliant orange-red starfish that came into the cove on a flow tide last September lay in the shallow tide pool in which he had taken residence, the only bright spot in a sea of mud and murky water. At first I thought that he was dead, but he had remained alive these several months when he could have gone out with the tide to safer quarters.

Each oyster on the pebbled beach hosted its load of limpets and clinging barnacles and some concealed a small black crab or two, no bigger than a ten-cent piece. At the mouth of the nameless creek that negotiates the cove in lazy loops and curls around the end of the spit to its final destination, half-buried sand dollars, relatives of long-spined sea urchins, stood on edge, their cilia moving to extract food particles from the water. Bleached skeletons of "dollars," their flower patterns clearly etched on dorsal surfaces, lay strewn about among empty, drilled shells of orange and white and striped snails and ribbed, heart-shaped cockles.

I came back to watch the tide begin its flow around the spit. Salt water seems to creep in slowly at first, meets fresh, curls and eddies; but then it picks up speed and becomes a tumbling rapid, as though bound by contract to fill the cove brim full before the next ebb begins. When the salt inflow had reached a foot or so in depth the first of the flounder

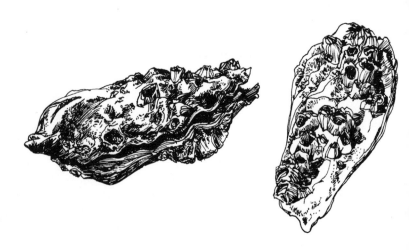

came. Aware of my presence on the bank, they darted forward, dropped to half-bury themselves in a cloud of sand for a long moment, and then darted ahead again. It is easy to confuse their forward progress with the moving shadows made by floating algae as the water deepens.

Sometimes schools of small silver fish enter with the incoming tide, nets of arrows as bright as needles. I always wonder whether they come into the cove to feed or if they are simply caught up accidentally and unable to resist the force of inflow. After the water has spread and deepened, I no longer see the flounder save sometimes as formless shapes magnified to look as big as stingrays. Gradually the fresh-water creek disappears, lost under salt water. The muddy dead brown skirts of encircling firs vanish and only green is left. On sunny days the full cove mirrors the old boathouse, the blue sky, the fringe of trees. On moonlit nights a field of stars lies drowned there.

Gray Fog

In January many mornings began with fog. The area that embraced the house and outbuildings was an island on an island, a vignette softened at the edges. A clammy gray blanket obscured the meadow, and a diaphanous silk mantle in shades of mauve veiled the water.

Throughout the mornings we heard the hoarse voices of the work boats as they groped their way down the inlet into Balch Passage and inched through the narrow channel between Eagle Reef and McNeil Island. The ferry *Islander* materialized like a homing ghost ship, drawn by the siren at the landing that wailed a warning. Bundled into heavy clothing, the sleepy school children drifted down the bridge to board the boat. Island children through the sixth grade attend school on McNeil and go at eight-thirty. The young in upper grades board the six-forty ferry for the mainland. To have gone to school by water would have seemed a true adventure when I was a child in Kansas. To sail to school is just routine with these. Island living is the only kind of life some of them have known.

We have our own weather signs. A foggy morning usually means a day without rain, even though the sun may not break through until after the lunchtime whistle sounds at the penitentiary compound across the way. On such mornings I often set out early for a brief walk along one of the shore roads.

To walk along a fogged-in road gives a pleasant lost feeling. I could hear, as I walked, the lonely tolling of the big bell on Eagle Island, placed there to mark the reef. A stake light on such a morning would not be seen. Crews on early steamers passing here read danger or safety during foggy times in echoes bounced off banks or buildings.

By the time I had reached the ruins of Johnson's Landing, where side- and stern-wheelers once stopped to wood and water up, the fog had cleared sufficiently to reveal distorted reflections in the water, though the sun was still a mere suggestion, a wan floating disk in an undelineated sky. Demarcation lines wavered and the walls of the penitentiary buildings leaned out of focus and proportion, hung upside down, detached from their foundation stones. A floating duck displayed two heads, one real, one mirrored, but which was which? The prison launch, pulling out from the McNeil dock, sailed on a cushion of air.

Along a sheltered shore, I found a pussy willow that had opened plump gray catkins with a touch of rose. More shrub than tree, these little *Salicaceae* during late winter months decorate sunny banks and roadsides. In a family of more than two hundred members, this *Salix* is a maverick. Tree books dismiss it as "small and scrubby" or ignore it altogether. But its silvery catkins herald spring, and it is an eager grower. Twigs that fall on moist receptive earth sprout and grow to a height of a foot or more in a single season.

When the pale sun broke through, the fog was gone suddenly, as though whisked away by a feather duster. I left the shore and climbed the hill, to where a grove of old cedars huddled together. Their reddish bark hung in strips and their heavy overhanging boughs interlaced, making warm dry rooms carpeted by a spongy cushion of accumulated needle drop. Worn deer trails led to the spot from all directions, and the earth felt warm to the touch, like beds just vacated. When I asked a veterinarian once whether animals in the wild likely suffered from arthritis as we do in later years, he said, "Of course they do. Their joints and bones after death give evidence."

One January day a Pacific varied thrush, the first of his species I had seen all winter, put in an appearance in the orchard. Strictly a winter bird here, he goes by a variety of "given" names—snow, mountain, winter, spotted, golden, swamp, Alaska, painted—all ending with the word "robin." A handsome fellow, with a deep orange vest, a jet-black necklace, and an orange eye stripe, he does move about with robinlike hops and runs. But unlike the robin, he expends more energy in defense of territory than in allaying appetite. We rarely see him until after New Year's. By late March he will have gone off to breeding grounds at higher altitudes. On winter nights he has a peculiar habit of squatting in the roads. When car lights strike he slants off owl-like into darker woods. Even by day he seeks the shadows. His favorite hiding place in the yard here is underneath the prickly overhanging limbs of the holly trees. I hear him more often than I see him, a prolonged ghostly whistle followed by a pause, and then another whistle, lower key. His melodious song, seldom heard save during nesting season and in less inclement weather, is a blend of notes on high and low pitches. Coming from concealment in some grove or thicket, it has an ethereal sweetness.

Of Seals and Otters

For days the water remained calm, a flat leaden sheet like a dead sea. And then one morning the surface was dyed green and brown with masses of unattached plankton. The dictionary defines the noun as "an aggregate of passively floating or drifting organisms," the Greek word *planktos* having to do with wandering. All morning the slow meandering tide line was marked by a parade of drift, split whip wrack, brown kelp floated by air bladders, the thick slices sawed from logs, which we call wood cookies, and deadheads almost totally submerged, a boatman's hidden menace.

On logs escaped from rafts and on entire floating trees washed from their moorings on crumbling banks by heavy rains, gulls and cormorants rode in tandem. An occasional bright herring or other fish broke the surface and described a series of loops like a skipping stone, to fall, finally, among the slowly circling ducks. It is said that ducks herd herring, round them up into a ball with the help of big fish that drive from below. In the still air, gulls had soared back and forth all morning like paper gliders. Now they converged, screaming, upon a small area where the water boiled with life. The owner of the bait boat, farther out, must have been watching through his glasses. For he, too, swung his craft slowly and got underway, his bow pointed in the direction of the harvest.

The sleek, round, earless head of a harbor (or hair) seal appeared and moved about over the unruffled surface like a floating beach ball followed by a V-shaped wake. He accorded me one curious glance from his long-lashed, dark brown eyes; but then I might have been a stone on the beach for all that he acknowledged me. His ragged whiskers and expressive eyes give him a kindly look. An old man of the sea, he tends his own affairs. He sank from sight, leaving scarcely a ripple, and came up quite close to where I sat.

His dark-splotched head shone wet. On land he hitches along leaving an odd drag mark in the mud, flanked by nailprints. In water he is streamlined, a graceful and powerful swimmer. During a visit to McNeil Island once I watched a colony of harbor seals at ease a little way off-shore on Gertrude Island in the shelter of Still Harbor. Taking wise advantage of the protection afforded by the federal penitentiary, seals breed and rear their young each year in safety there. The previous year's pups, I noted, were still spotted with light yellow. While their elders slept or took the sun, the pups played in and out of the shallow water.

In the belief that they accounted for too many salmon (and for the bounty offered), harbor seals were once taken by the hundreds in the state of Washington. A wounded seal dives, one young hunter told me, and the water is obscured with blood for yards around, making it difficult to locate the victim. When the animals began to grow scarce in number, the bounty offer was withdrawn and belated research began. Of one hundred seal stomachs opened, only *two* contained salmon. The seals had fed on tomcod, herring, flounder, skate, octopus, shrimp, crab, starfish. Legislation was proposed and then enacted for harbor seal protection. Numbers again are on the increase.

One foggy winter morning our neighbor Hallie Green looked out through a window of her house high above the water and saw a parade of animals "as large as Collie dogs" humping awkwardly along in a line in the direction of Lake Florence. Glossy-coated, dark, and wet looking, they moved "like a caravan of camels," as she described them.

Hallie's husband Carlo readily identified the ungraceful pedestrians as river otters and surmised that the animals had crossed the channel from the mainland or from a neighboring island and had made their way up the long sloping ravine with some instinctive knowledge that a body of fresh water could be found above.

The arrival of any creature previously unseen here creates a little stir on the Island and word spreads rapidly. Pressed for details, Hallie drew a sketch that dovetailed with those in guidebooks—broad, flat head, short ears, small eyes, heavy long tail, wide muzzle, short legs designed for swimming, not for walking. Many of us made fruitless pilgrimages, looked along the lakeshores for tracks or mudslides. River otters, members of the weasel family (which animal they resemble save for larger size), feed on fish and frogs. In spring, females produce three to five young, in nests dug into banks and lined with sticks and leaves.

In January a pair of otters was sighted by Island boys, who mistook them at first for harbor seals. A single otter was later seen in nearby Lake Josephine, and there were other sighting reports or rumors. One was seen to rise and take his ease on a lake float. Presumably, some or all of the animals seen by Hallie remain in one lake or the other, but I have yet to see one.

For the most part, lakeshores are far too shallow for the mudslides otters seem to make for fun and coasting games. Sticks and stones that might injure flesh are carefully removed and toboggan tracks kept wet. Folding webbed feet backward, these comical animals move forward on their bellies, like children on sled runners. Hind feet serve as rudders. The coasters splash headfirst into the water, emerge dripping wet, and climb the bank to repeat the run.

More recently, a few sea otters (*Enhydra lutris*) have been seen offshore in salt water by various Islanders, especially in Amsterdam and Oro bays on opposite sides of the Island. Long believed to be on the brink of extinction, these floaters and back-swimmers have been re-established along Northwest coasts through the patient efforts of their former enemy, man, who killed them for their handsome and valuable pelts. No sea otter has ever been reported in a fresh-water stream or lake.

Offshore, here, they lie on floats to groom their rich, dense fur with extended claws. Or they recline on their backs in the water, extract food previously collected into foreleg pouches, and feed from their chests, employed as tables. One Islander reported seeing an otter use a stone held in a forepaw to break the shell of a clam or mussel placed on his chest.

Snow

Shortly after New Year's Day 1969 a quiet snow began, and continued to depths and duration hardly remembered here. Big soft flakes, like goose down, whitened roads and roofs in moments, weighted boughs and stood in sculptured mounds on fence post and mailbox, to gentle every harsh or ugly contour. Accustomed, after more than two decades, to comparatively mild Puget Sound winters, we ourselves had almost forgotten snows of blizzard consistency. We filled the bird feeders and watched through the windows with a certain happy and selfish nostalgia. We had no need to travel. The snow would rain out presently; or a wet "chinook" would come to relieve us, one of those moist southwest winds that laps up snow along the Washington and Oregon coast and leaves dry earth within an hour or so. Although I have been witness to a few of these phenomenal zephyrs since coming to the Northwest in 1946, I still consider them to be a kind of miracle.

Days passed, and the silent snowfall continued, filled wood-lined roads, obliterated fences, and drifted deep against the buildings. Birds came in flocks. Sharp-billed starlings in speckled plumage swaggered along the fence rails, and fed with purple finches, towhees, sparrows, brown-headed cowbirds, and countless juncos. Crested

Steller's jay came, an incredible black and deep blue in a world of white. Robins and varied thrushes set upon apples brought from storage. Downy woodpeckers, male and female look-alikes, shared suet and bacon dripping with chestnut-backed and black-capped chickadees.

The air was filled with chickadee music, the "dee, dee, dee" of black-caps, the lisping of the chestnut-backed. They sounded gay and exuberant, as though they loved the snow. In the high tops of the fir trees they hung upside down and swung on brown cone clusters. I stirred up "chickadee pudding" from a recipe I had seen somewhere—bacon and beef dripping, peanut butter, raisins, cornmeal, chopped apple, crumbs from the cookie jar and the cracker box. I hauled out big Oregon pine cones saved from Christmas and spread them thick with peanut butter laced with cornmeal and set them in the snow. In an hour they were picked clean and customers sat about, waiting.

The string bag of suet I had suspended from a tree limb vanished in the night. Telltale tracks of raccoons, like baby handprints, patterned the snow underneath the limb and led to an aperture underneath the chicken house. I filled a small wire basket with the fat and hung it from an eave trough of the bathroom lean-to, inaccessible, I thought, from roof above or earth below. A downy woodpecker and a host of purple finches took turns throughout the day with a Steller's jay that tried in vain to gain a foothold.

As I sat at my typewriter late that evening, I became gradually aware of a recurrent clicking sound in the vicinity of the back door, and stepped outside, armed with a flashlight.

His hind feet clamped precariously on the trough, a half-grown raccoon hung from the bathroom eave. One forefoot held the basket on its string. With the nails of his other forefoot he painstakingly picked bits of fat from between the meshes. Confused by my appearance, he let the basket go and it clicked against the siding, the sound I had been hearing. Hanging upside down, he peered near-sightedly at the light and then swung like a plum bob in an effort to regain his balance.

For a moment I was sure he would not make it and prepared to catch him in my arms to break the fall. But he did a quick mid-air gyration and landed on the eave. Obviously reluctant to take his leave, he held his ground for a time, the while he tried to stare me down or challenge my intrusion. But then he turned his back and began the long slippery climb up the snowy shingles to the ridgepole.

By daylight his plantigrade tracks were plain. They flowed over the ridgepole and down the other side and continued from the base of the pine tree by means of which he had reached earth again. Crossing the yard and descending the beach steps, the tracks ended, surprisingly, at the water line.

I moved the metal basket to the clothes line and hung it high at dead center. Only a tightrope walker, or winged raccoon, I thought triumphantly, could reach it there. But after two nights the basket disappeared, and I never found it. I could only conclude that one masked marauder had stood on another's shoulders.

The wide overhang extension of the corrugated metal roof that covers the chicken house, a surface glazed with ice those snowy nights, provided a final answer. But, in truth, I felt a trifle guilty. From our beds, after dark, we heard the long slide, the heavy thud, the grunts and growls of pain, or protest. In the morning and for all the days afterward, the basket suspended from the roof's edge remained untouched save by the daytime patrons for which it was intended.

For all his charm of manner and appearance, a raccoon is an incurable glutton. A family of raccoons can strip a pear or plum tree of an entire season's crop in a single night, and does, often. Our only recourse is to harvest slightly green fruit. To add insult to gluttony, the cheeky

raiders leave their droppings at the feast. Scat looks un-
digested, as though the food consumed in haste had gone
through the coarse plate of a food mill. I find odoriferous
mounds filled with seeds and unassimilated matter on the
broad limbs of trees, defiling the bird bath and the garden
chairs, once in copious quantities on my husband's work-
bench. For some odd reason, beachcombing raccoons leave
disgusting heaps of offal on beach steps and landing. No
panacea I have tried serves as even a temporary deterrent.

The logic behind this repulsive practice lies beyond my
comprehension. This is not a clam nor oyster beach. The
shore here holds little in the way of food until the various
berries ripen along the bank. Where these offenders pass
their days and sleep off their glut I have no notion. A beaten
'coon path flanks the holly trees, runs underneath the board
fence, and crosses the road ditch to the stairhead. At the
foot of the steps tracks take up again in damp sand but
disappear among the cobbles.

In an effort at useful recycling this past spring I inadvertently provided a fresh food source for these nocturnal
gourmets. Layers of newspapers topped with old hay
proved, to my satisfaction, a housing project for a host of
fat earthworms. One morning the beds presented an unsightly shambles of plowed-up hay and wet newsprint.
Scarcely a worm survived the night's feasting.

Jackpines and Oak Apples

Mercury that had plummeted to nearly record lows
began a slow rise. Blue-black clouds obscured the snow-
covered Olympic and Cascade ranges. During the night
we heard on the rooftop the first welcome patter of rain-
drops. The following morning, roads along salt water were
nearly bare of snow. Leaves of madroña and rhododendrons

that had hung stiff and black stood out crisp and green again as though by some internal magic.

In deep woods sheltered from rain and sun, the drifts melted slowly and revealed the storm's toll. Boughs of fir and cedar and hemlock sprawled, prostrate, among flattened collapsed fronds of sword and deer fern. Shallow-rooted trees had gone down by the hundreds or reclined among outstretched limbs of neighboring trees, where they would remain alive for years but never stand erect again. Entire root systems of the fallen stood on edge, exposed, long muddy claws clutching rocks and balls of snow. Among the spongy duff of centuries, the earth was pitted with muddy cavities.

Along the road to Oro Bay, melting drifts revealed less perishable litter in the form of unsightly heaps of soft drink cans and bottles, foil, and plastic. During the past year, numerous direction markers to Island disposal pits have been changed to County Sanitary Fill, a more sophisticated but no more effective phrase than the homely admonition County Dump that formerly graced the roads. The change proved baffling to our beginning reader, Lael. Puzzled by the bright new lettering during a walk one day from Higgins Cove to Villa Beach, she took a wrong turn and was half-way to Otso Point before she discovered her navigation error.

During such foul-weather spells as the January snow, we more than ever appreciate Lyle Carlson's store on Oro Bay, a cache besieged by Islanders as soon as the roads had cleared sufficiently to allow for easy transit. The road to Lyle's store skirts the long tongue of bay where the clear fresh waters of Schoolhouse Creek meet and mingle with incoming salt water at flow tide.

At the edge of the woods, where the two environments of woods and marsh (or meadow) meet, the pines we call (not quite correctly) "jackpines" crowd together against the denser backdrop of cedar, fir, and hemlock. These are my favorite conifers here. The long two-ranked needles have sometimes a blue, sometimes a yellowish-green tinge. Small egg-shaped cones are strongboxes to shield the seeds. It is said that seeds in cone cases frequently survive the fiercest forest fires and that they burst out later into cooled ashes to sprout and begin new forest growth.

For some reason to do with moisture, soil content, or seed distribution, pines spring up as thick as alder seedlings in the low area between Oro and Amsterdam bays and grow sparsely elsewhere on the Island. Throughout the winter, chickadees ransack the spiny cones, which serve as stocked chipmunk cupboards during summer months. Cones ripen late in August, or September. In early spring the trees are decorated with sticky, upstanding, candle-like cylinders topped by tiny crimson burrs, along with masses of yellow male flowers that release clouds of pollen at the slightest disturbance.

That morning after snow melt, I turned off the old Ekenstam-Johnson Road at the head of Oro Bay to follow a narrow road cut through second growth, where moisture-loving plants such as speedwell and monkey flower and orange and yellow columbines like dainty ballet dancers crowd the ditches each early summer. None of these were showing in January, of course. But cat-tails with long brown velvet heads stood tall on either side, and as far as the eye could see rank sword ferns and salal and huckleberry made the undergrowth a jungle.

Beyond the end of the road, where a farm has been cleared, a white oak tree grows alone near the shore of East Oro Bay, an old tree with massive crown and heavy gnarled limbs encrusted with gray lichen. Each fall and winter and throughout most of the spring months, the tree is hung thickly with a false fruiting of "oak apples," silvery nutlike excrescences caused by egg deposits of gall wasps or flies. Such an oak may live three hundred years or more, authorities say. This one was hung with shining egg-sized "apples" when I first saw it more than twenty years ago. The galls appear to inhibit the tree no more than does the lichen, nonflowering thallophyte composed of fungi in symbiotic union with an alga. Galls serve as houses, cradles, prisons if you will, for little gall wasp larvae.

Each year I pluck a gall or two to carry home, hoping to witness the miracle of life emerging. I never have. I find the pinhole exits, the tiny tunnels, but I miss the debut. Where do the metamorphosed go? I have kept galls for years, along with old gourds, cones, buckeye seeds. Once I sliced a gall as large as a baseball. It was all "cork" except for one crescent-curved chamber no bigger than half a thumbnail. There the prisoner slept, a curled white grub half as long as his enclosure. The shape he might have taken remained a mystery. I lacked the power to put the gall back together. Piqued by curiosity, or lack of faith, I had aborted the cycle. The larva died.

Galls sometimes go by the name of "*morbid* oak apples." Unwholesome? Tainted? Corrupted? But these lumps of swollen tissue are a source of tannic acid used in inks and dyeing. Oak apples are imported from exotic places—Aleppo, Tripoli, Smyrna. Or so I've read.

A line in *Insects** reads, "Insect galls are not well understood." Drawings show an oak apple, a goldenrod gall, spindle-shaped, a grape-like growth on blackberry. Woolly galls grow on oak *leaves*. For all our study, how much in nature remains unsolved enigma? What instinct drives the salamander unerringly to breeding ground? What motivation prompts the gall wasp, the migratory bird? What kind of clock times the odyssey of seeds and spiders?

* A Golden Nature Guide by Herbert Zim and Clarence Cottam (New York: Simon and Schuster, 1951).

The Eagle and the Salmon

Late one afternoon I stood on the shore below Lake Josephine and watched a bald eagle describe high wide circles against the sparkling sunlit backdrop of Mount Rainier. How did the bald eagle come by his name? He is not bald at all; he wears a lovely, loose-fitting helmet of white feathers. To my earthbound mind he had a wild free look, and I knew a twinge of almost envy until I remembered his precarious position.

When we first came to the Island, the bluff near the lake, with its heavy growth of trees and tall charred snags, was a natural game habitat, visited only rarely by the few Islanders who made their way along the rough access trail to fish or hunt ducks, to gather brush or firewood, or to pick the wild berries that grew in profusion in cutover clearings. Bald eagles built big stick nests in the tall trees and set up watch above the shore on high dead pinnacles. We saw them often, then. We rarely see them now. Indeed, we are told that no more than thirty-five hundred of these great birds remain in the United States outside the state of Alaska.

Like the sea gull, the eagle renders valuable service by keeping shores clean of dead and dying fish. But he is something more than a disposal aide. Even more poignant than the silent soaring of white gulls over blue water, his wild free flight is poetry in motion. His fierce eyes are telescopic. His feathers weigh twice as much as does his framework. His cry, heard during the nesting season, is a lonely "pleek," softer and more appealing than the remembered echoing scream of the golden eagle over Colorado canyons. This one soared in silence, and went so high finally that he was lost from sight.

Years ago a member of the ferry crew told of watching a

pair of these enormous birds in flight in the direction of the bluff that borders on the lakes here. The larger of the two bore a big salmon with which he seemed to be struggling. He lost altitude, flapped his wings rapidly as though in a desperate effort to recover, but was obviously forced lower by the weight of his burden. But then, as though at some signal, the companion bird, which the watcher took to be the female, swept directly underneath with deep accelerated strokes. The exhausted flier let the fish drop. His companion caught it deftly, and the pair crossed the shore line and moved out of sight among the trees that clothed the nesting grounds.

February

Harbingers

By the first of February spring was in the air, but the earth remained cold and soggy. We called it boot weather. People said, "If you can't see the mountain it's going to rain. If you can see the mountain it's already raining." If the day began with fog we might see the sun. If the day began with sun, it would end with rain. Evening gray and morning red came near to being true proverb. We shrugged and said, "Rain's better than snow." At least days had lengthened. The air smelled of spring.

Rain fell for a week without letup, turned to mist, to drizzle, to rain again. A blue haze hung over the water. The mainland, even McNeil Island, were indistinct blurs on the horizon, sometimes blue, sometimes gray. The horizon advanced and receded and advanced.

24

Attacked by cabin fever, jaded by artificial lights, I put on boots and rain gear and went out each afternoon in search of spring. I slogged down an old logging road to a clearing where the last of the portable sawmills had set up to process usable second growth. For as long as the waste slab remained firm, Islanders had carted it away to use as fuel. Now the heap had shrunk to a mound of wet, decayed trimmings blanketed by a tangle of honeysuckle and trailing wild blackberry. A few dried berries still clung to briars among new swollen buds. Clumps of dark-brown, hooded helvella, a fungus with thin folded skin, little saddles, found nourishment in blackened sawdust. From one of these a slug had nibbled a corner. But a slug is not to be trusted. Helvella stands accused of several cases of lethal poisoning. "It is better not to experiment. Never taste this mushroom raw." So say the books. I was not tempted. A blackened stump was surrounded completely by woody polypores, tier upon tier, diminutive brackets arranged in rows, like empty seats in a circus tent.

Distracted by a blue flash, I watched a Steller's jay jerk his way among the feathered green of a fir. Cheeky and excitable, thievish and aggressive, he shouts in syllables of three, a raucous "shaak shaak shaak." But he enlivens a day with the most beautiful shade in the range of blues. One jay's favorite tree is a tall fir on which limbs have been reduced to stubs that form a natural ladder. Alighting on the lowest, he ascends step by step like a soft-shoe dancer, shouting and spiraling, and comes back to repeat the stunt.

Noisy in the woods, the jay comes like a sneak thief to the feeder. Lesser occupants depart in haste. Raspberry-dipped finches, the black and orange towhee, the mouse-brown sparrows, sleek and jumpy juncos stand aside. The jay rarely eats. He flies away to tuck the corn into some crevice between rail and post, behind a loose fleck of bark, beneath a fallen leaf. Like a miser or a kleptomaniac, he hoards without reason. I have yet to see him return to one of these caches.

I watched a rusty sparrow routed from the feeder by a jay. He sat on a limb of the Transparent apple tree, quiet and watchful. When the jay had gone, the little bird dropped, plucked a leaf aside, and enjoyed the spoils. The jay himself backs away when confronted by the sharp sword of a red-shafted flicker, a bully put down, a biter bitten. I always feel a little sorry, or embarrassed, for him.

One day I came home along a deer trail that wore a green moss carpet. Deer step so lightly as hardly to disturb the moss. Where the trail crossed a muddy winter branch, the earth was marked with heart-shaped prints of various sizes. A fawn had been here, left a print little larger than a silver dollar. I knelt, and discovered for a second time a wide, cat-like track too big to have been made by any domestic feline. We first saw the track last winter. Book in hand, we took careful measurements, but came to no firm conclusion. I looked up the gulch. That jungle could hide a dozen bobcats, wildcats, tigers even.

Beyond the creek crossing, I stopped to watch a pair of cedar waxwings that moved from branch to branch and

kept up a sibilant whispering. The waxy cinnamon brown on their wing coverts shone like satin. We rarely see these birds around the house. In summer they may come, all at once, in swiftly moving restless flocks, to feast on tritoma bloom. They come in autumn for ripened holly berries on occasion, for firethorn or hawthorn or cotoneaster. In February they move singly or in pairs, usually in silence.

The trail entered a clearing, a grown-around homestead, long since abandoned. The house was two-story, with a lean-to kitchen. One window was framed with squares of colored glass, still intact. The roof was filled with holes, but smothered under Himalaya blackberry vines, long runners poking thorny fingers inside through holes in broken siding. A tall leaning alder blocked the doorway. In one corner a molded glove and a runover shoe still held the shape of the hand, the foot of their owners. Did the same wear both? A big man, surely. The stiffened glove was enormous. Even a teenager who lived there would likely be dead by now. A hole in the floor underneath the kitchen disclosed empty Mason jars, bits of broken flowered china.

I heeded my own often repeated warning, "Watch out for old wells." There must have been a well somewhere. Cedar posts and fallen pickets marked a small enclosure off toward the wood. Each post held aloft a mound of bright moss topped by lidded, spore-filled capsules, like candles on a birthday cake. One mound nourished a six-inch hemlock seedling. Another, surprisingly, cradled a limpet shell. How had a limpet shell come here? In an ancient dump I found a five-inch brass harness buckle, a handful of bright glass buttons such as studded harness straps. "No farmer here could afford that kind of gim-crack," a native told me. And then remembered, "But we had a man here who sometimes drove team for a Tacoma brewery."

An old and broken pear tree, lost in alders, still held living buds swollen in response to one more spring. Along

a fir log, brown, crumbling, and moss coated, a new forest
had begun—fir, cedar, hemlock, maple, deer and lady
ferns, the delicate, bare, angled stems of red huckleberry.

Beyond that was jungle. Lost temporarily in a tangle of
wild growth that even the deer avoided, I fought my
way through winter-bare thimbleberry and thorny, blue-
stemmed blackcap, out to the road again. A bit of rusted
gate remained. This line of jungle had been the driveway,
the access road, the way out and in. A fallen tree, gone
down in some earlier winter storm, presented a clay-en-
crusted root like a solid wall, a hanging garden clothed
with sword ferns. From where I stood no trace of the house
was visible.

"Tansy" Ragwort

Running the fence line in search of breaks, on the tenth
of February, I was surprised to see a tall clump of golden
ragwort that had survived the storm and was still bravely
blooming in the shelter of a wild hazel tree in Neighbor
Buchanan's pasture. This is the rogue *Senecio,* dire villain
whose cumulative poison is said to bring quick death to
livestock, which may become addicted to its taste.

When, a few years ago, warning posters first appeared,
identifying the species, we took pains to root out each plant
that showed. We pulled and burned every specimen on
our own premises and stopped along roads to bring ragwort
home in bundles for careful incineration. And still it
throve. It is said that a single vigorous individual of this
particular *Senecio* throws out between six thousand and
ten thousand seeds and that no known herbicide is more
than partially successful in its eradication. Furthermore,
the plant has no natural enemies, at least in western Washington, where it has gained a rapid foothold. In fields
where other forage is available, grazing animals usually

leave the plant alone. Even when close-cropped pasture land turns brown in August, I have observed, standing plants of golden ragwort remain untouched. But the risk is there.

Then came a story by Hill Williams, science editor of the *Seattle Times*, to reveal that a certain French moth named Cinnabar, brought from France as an experiment, eats *only* "tansy ragwort," and that an Italian flea beetle, likewise imported for the purpose, bores into the root crown of this particular *Senecio*. The question is: Will these Samaritans adapt to the idiosyncrasies of western Washington climate?

Since their initial appearance, the warning posters have puzzled me. Only one guidebook I have found refers to this poisonous but rather handsome plant as "tansy ragwort." Flowers of true tansy (*Tanacetum*) are golden buttons, clusters of yellow disk flowers with a strong smell of lemon. Ragwort has a similar leaf but not so finely cut. Tansy is a composite grown in British cottage gardens for use in cooking and as tonic. True tansy grows thick along the railroad grade beside the ferry dock in Steilacoom across the channel and may grow here. But I have never seen a specimen on the Island.

So far as I know, the solitary hazel that stands alone in the pasture here has never borne a nut. Perhaps it needs a companion tree. In February its ragged upper branches are hung with long cream-yellow catkins, but all of the lower branches are dead and bare, browsed year after year by deer and cattle that shelter there from sun and rain. Where this slender birch must compete with alder (which it resembles at an early stage), it is little more than shrub. Along the trail to the old ram at Higgins Cove hazels grow with vigor and produce nuts in whiskered cases, back to back and shaped like an acorn cup. Jays and chipmunks love the nuts. Wild hazel and orchard filbert are the same *Corylus* genus and differ little, save that the latter is tree instead of shrub. Nuts are said to ripen by August 22, St. Philbert's Day. Hence the name "filbert." But who was St. Philbert? And why should he have had a day? I looked among the saints but could not find him.

Above and beyond the hazel tree stands the half-buried reservoir that supplies this house with water from a dug well, a developed spring, hidden in an alder thicket. When the reservoir was new, the concrete wall showed plainly against the green slope of meadow. These years it is mossed over, the roof weathered. Each year the alder trees creep forward. I can hardly find the well now. The board cover is buried deep beneath a mound of opportunist Himalaya.

At first we tried to keep the place neat by taking out the alder seedlings as they sprang up around the well. But each time the trees were cut the water supply dwindled until new trees came to shade the area, to hold the moisture. Now we let the alders grow. The earth around the well above the reservoir is bog, black and rich and filled with moisture-loving growth. Sword ferns splay out among the Himalayas. Spathes and spadices of skunk cabbage scent the air and cover the earth with golden candles.

One February day I found a stranger here, a tiny plant with finely cut foliage. Believing it to be some kind of corydalis, of which bleeding heart and Dutchman's breeches are the better-known species, I dug the specimen and brought it home to set in the rock wall where I could watch it.

The first flowering came in April among cascades of leaves, a terminal raceme of sulphur-yellow, spurred flowers. From then until October the plant was never without blossoms. As happens fairly frequently, the search for identification ended in a favorite book, William Stevens' *Kansas Wild Flowers*. The plant is *Corydalis aurea*, western golden corydalis. By what route had it come here? By what routes, indeed, have all the species come to this once barren mass of rock and rubble?

February Voices

Nights became milder but remained wet. A chorus of frog song arose from wet shrubbery and from growth-choked gulches. Sorting out a single voice, I tried to approach sufficiently close to see the singer. I stole forward, stopped, listened, changed direction, and stood deceived. Occasionally a small greenish form leapt from underfoot, to disappear in some bush or grass clump. But usually the voice simply fell silent, and took up again when I was back inside. Occasionally, by day, we heard a different, deeper, more guttural and less musical croak from beneath the floorboards. A descendant perhaps of the two dozen toads transplanted years ago from Kansas? More than once I braved cobwebs that hang like a maze of net across the "crawl space" underneath the kitchen. The phrase "crawl space" is used literally. My careful approach was fruitless here, too, and I was back on the ground floor combing cobwebs out of my hair when the refrain began again.

As spring deepened the rich warbling song of purple finches came from pine and fir and holly trees. When rain ceased to fall they sang in the open, from the still bare boughs of the weeping willow or from the power wires. Between performances they ticked in and out of the poultry house to feed on the leftover sunflower heads hung up last fall for drying. Presently only husks were left, round clusters of empty cells, like drained-out honey comb.

"Cherry bird," an Islander calls the purple finch, because of its liking for the green beginnings of fruit. A flock of finches will alight in a blossoming cherry tree and feast unseen, creating a literal rain of blossoms. But they account, too, for a nice quantity of thistle and dandelion and other pest seeds, and a finch's singing voice is hardly surpassed from so small a set of vocal chords.

On misty nights as I walked down the quarter mile of road after supper to pick up the *Tacoma News Tribune*, brought across each weekday evening on the ferry, I heard the lonely-sounding overhead cry of a solitary unseen killdeer. A noisy plover, appropriately named *Charadrius vociferus*, the killdeer, often called the "killdee," is a country bird, a lover of plowed fields and a shallows wader. In Kansas pastures he hung around the ponds. Here he frequents beaches. In flight he wears a bordered cape in black and white. His double neck bands are jet black.

He doesn't *build* a nest, he scrapes a nest together, a few collected stones on bare plowed earth if he can find it. Buff spotted eggs lie unprotected and hardly camouflaged. But he does his best to dupe a possible marauder by putting on an elaborate ploy of being broken-winged, dragging and crying across a field in an effort to lure the intruder away from his potential victim. He is an earth bird, a running bird. One of his favorite paths is the road that passes in front of our house. I like to watch his halting progress. He runs rapidly for a few steps, then stops abruptly, stands stock still for a few seconds, and then repeats the performance, like a school boy in a game of cheese-it.

One pitch-black night in February I heard the long-drawn yodeling of a loon, an eerie sound not often experienced here. Except when driven in from the coast by Pacific storms, these big dagger-billed birds come rarely to Puget Sound, and then only as brief winter visitors. Save in breeding waters, they remain, generally, silent. Breeding grounds are in the far North, in the Aleutians or the northern Yukon, less frequently along the ocean coast. This one remained unseen, a disembodied voice, far out. But we do see them here upon occasion, and I never tire of watching.

Thick-necked and long-bodied, a loon looks enormous

when magnified by his own reflection in the water. His food consists mainly of fish, for which he dives, sometimes to a depth, it is said, of two hundred feet or better. I do not know how long he can remain submerged: I have given up a time or two while waiting for him to surface.

The loons we see sometimes in winter or early spring rarely show the necklaces they wear with summer plumage, though they may show a trace. I often wonder who started the rumor that a loon laughs. His quavering falsetto arising at night from black water has an effect of wailing, as of unseen people mourning from a hilltop for their dead. Thoreau referred to the loon's call as "semi-human."

A young boy here told of seeing one of these big birds jerking about in an odd fashion a little way offshore, as though somehow entrapped. Disregarding the cold water, the boy stepped out of his clothing and plunged in to try to effect a rescue. He was forced to beat a hasty retreat when the loon swam to attack, its dagger bill spread and great wings lifted as though to thrash the boy under.

Sulphur and Molasses Time

The new growth that crowned madroña stumps was pruned each night by deer, half a leaf here, half a leaf there, until only stems remained. Last November's hunter and his guns forgotten, deer appeared in numbers in the roads of evenings and early mornings. Bucks and does, along with last year's fawns, emerged from the woods at dusk, grazed peaceably on the meadows. Man is the deer's only enemy here, if you discount stray dogs.

The animals seemed painfully thin. Some said the uncommonly hard freeze, the prolonged snow had taken its toll among the old and young. Yearlings had lost their spots, turned dark, and donned winter coats. But they stayed fawn size and ribby. "They gorge on new growth in

spring, and scour," one old-timer told me, victims not of
scarcity but of plenty.

No matter how chill the wind and the rain, the feel, the
smell of spring was there, the slow steady stir of new life
beginning. Fresh signs appeared each day. Circinate fronds
of sword fern that had clustered at the base of last year's
growth like eggs in a nest began to uncurl and loosen.
Mounds of wet brown leaves were moved aside to reveal
matted rosettes of buttercups and flat velvet leaves of awak-
ening foxglove. Indian plum would be the first of the
shrubs to bloom. Other names are "oso-berry," "bird cherry,"
Osmaronia cerasiformis. Next would come red-flower currant. I watched these tall marginal shrubs for signs of swollen buds opening.

Winter still held on Island beaches. A chill came up
from wet stones, and water reflected gray skies. A line of
somber cormorants (Islanders call them "shags") floated by
on a log, carried by the tide. I cannot distinguish one cormorant from another, nor male from female. Kitchin says
Anderson Island has Baird's and Brandt's, *pelagicus* and
penicillatus, but only as winter visitors, and that they breed
along the ocean coast. Sitting or swimming, the big blackish birds present an odd snaky appearance. These sat as
though carved to the perch, a macabre wooden row, unaware of the passing scene.

But then one lurched forward and down, came up with
a struggling fish which he swallowed at a gulp, and resumed his place beside his imperturbable companions.
Surely of all the birds in the world only the turkey buzzard
is less lovely to look at. They sit with hook-tipped bills up-
lifted. Their rare communications, which consist of unpleasant grunts and croaks, are distinctly unmusical. Their
one claim to grace comes of their occasional spread-eagle
pose, a position taken, it is theorized, to dry their wings
following a dive.

Farther out, glaucous-winged gulls rode among debris

that marked the tide line, or wheeled on set wings above the sullen water. A flotilla of dark ducks, too far away to identify, floated among the drift, and a thin-necked grebe turned a somersault and vanished. (Grebes, too, are only winter visitors here.) A patient little tugboat with a wide log tow waited for the tide to turn in its favor. A late sun whitened the cratered peak of Mount Rainier and shone on the pale-buff penitentiary buildings, but the Island lay in shadow.

As though on cue, the coromorants took off and formed a pointed wedge close above the surface. The wheeling gulls dropped one by one like leaves to settle on the log raft. The patch of sunlight widened to blanket the miniature white houses on the mainland and colored the water a sudden vivid blue laced with coral, then dropped behind the mountains. Bird by bird, like a counting-out rhyme, the ducks went under.

Robins

On bright days during the winter months the woods were open and inviting. Last year's birds' nests hung exposed. After the fall defoliation of deciduous shrubs and trees and the going over of bracken fern and nettle, the forest takes on a third dimension, a depth of perspective, until lush spring growth once more draws a green curtain. Intermittent cold rain continued, but hills and roadsides colored slowly with tinted, enlarged buds, and alder boughs reddened against the still somber green of conifers. Massive limbs of broadleaf maple, clothed in moss and lichen, wore ornamental cloaks of lady ferns and polypody.

Sometimes the sun emerged like a blessing, to shine for an hour and turn wet boughs to silver. Globes of water clung and glistened on every twig like drops of syrup on a spoon, each globe a prism. Fields and woods steamed. Madroña boles glowed cinnamon pink. Big olive-green banana slugs, slow-moving gastropods, came out of hiding. As I walked along the road one morning a winter wren trilled from concealment in the huckleberry border. The leaves stirred with his weight, and he made a ticking sound. I thought of E. B. White's response to the question as to whether he watched birds. "Yes," he said. "And they watch me."

Underneath a Spitzenberg apple tree on the slope we dignify by the name of orchard, the neighbor's cat crouched close to the earth, his one good eye, gold-green, fixed on a robin, busy with a desiccated apple. Now and then the robin paused at his work to acknowledge the cat's presence by a sharp look. But the cat is old and slow, and it was plain that the robin held him in contempt. Only nostalgia, or pretense, kept the cat on the cold, wet grass when he might have been curled up behind a warm stove. Like an old man on a park bench who eyes the girls in miniskirts, he watched the robin. He knew the bird was unattainable, and in truth he did not much desire it. But inside the cells of his aging brain a memory stirred, he knew he *ought* to want it.

Bird fancier though I am, I confess to a certain lack of rapport with robins. I find their cheerful chirping unmelodious and sometimes monotonous, and too optimistic for early morning. Guidebooks praise the robin as accounting for a host of insect pests. Ours seem to have an appetite only for fruit and angleworms. During each year we have two sets of robins. Some say our summer birds are of a larger size and that they have a distinctive eye stripe, but they all look alike to me. One contingent, the winter birds, arrives in noisy flocks about November, to strip the holly trees before the Christmas rush and to feast on winter apples, and moves back north before the equinox. Summer resident birds, identical so far as I can see, appear in April, construct untidy nests, rear two broods of gawky, speckled young, and leave us in September. Anderson Island resident birds in winter, according to ornithologist E. A. Kitchin, are "visitants from the north."

Turdus migratorius by scientific name, the robin is cousin to the other thrushes. The young of all the thrush family have speckled breasts. "Typical" thrushes migrate at night; robins migrate, in flocks, by day. The thrush we called the bluebird nests in cavities. Robins and other thrushes build in trees and shrubs. A robin's nest looks not so much built as thrown together. Her eggs are "robin's egg blue" in color, a phrase used by fashion designers and manufacturers of car bodies to describe a color neither blue nor green, but somehow both. Admirers prejudiced in robins' favor declare the birds to be "fine singers," and I am bound to admit that a spring without their cheerful "blu-rp! blur-p" would be too quiet. Even the "tut, tut, tut" of *winter* robins breaks the silence with a certain promise.

I was fully grown before I learned that a robin was a thrush and that our "brown thrush" in southeastern Kansas was not thrush but thrasher. We gave our own names to native fauna as well as flora, and they suited us. The "butcher bird" impaled lesser birds and mice on thorns of Osage orange. His real name was shrike, or *Lanius,* but he was a black-masked butcher of evil habit, as his name described. The bobwhite named himself. A catbird really mewed. The cardinal was "the redbird."

Likewise, we had our own voice interpretations. The redbird asked, "What cheer?" in loud, clear children's language. (My husband Earle believes to this day that *their* redbirds called, "Sweet Earle!") The meadowlark, or skybird, was my all-time favorite. We see and hear him here occasionally. A denizen of open fields, he tossed his whistled notes aloft, an aerial melody that seemed to come from all directions, that wreathed our heads as we hurried to school across the dew-wet meadow. I can never disassociate the memory of that rural (Pinkston) school, where I entered first grade and later taught eight grades, from a certain nostalgia for his morning aria.

A Kansas friend, who also grew up in meadowlark country, tells of a spirited discussion between two factions of young interpreters. To one, the bright yellow and black and white bird shrilled a derisive, "Your green petticoat's a'showin'." To the others, his flute-like whistle announced good news, "Here comes spring just a'leggin' it off!"

On breathless summer nights in Kansas, the "rain crow's" toneless melody sounded from dark, dry thickets. Was he, in reality, *Coccyzus,* the yellow-billed cuckoo? To my knowledge, I never saw him. In times of devastating drouth he betrayed us often. But, prophet false or true, he often gave us courage.

Rain

When rain falls without cessation, it is easy to forget a country where all signs failed "in dry weather." One who has never lived without sufficient water for even the most essential uses cannot conceive of what it means to be deprived of this so simple blessing. Or so I tell myself each winter when I may be inclined to complain of water surfeit. I am still haunted by the remembered sound of thirsty bawling cattle.

From the farm in Kansas, where ponds and creeks and wells dried up too many summers, I moved to north-central Oklahoma, where the muddy river that supplied the town was frequently reduced to stagnant pools. "Puget Sound country," an Oklahoma woman shuddered when she heard that we proposed to make the move. "People dry their clothes on porches. I spent a winter there."

And so they did, I found, in pre-automatic-dryer days, and still do. But barring the small inconveniences rain may bring, I have come to like the rainy seasons, especially on this Island. We dress for rain. I suspect that the split vamp, rubber-soled boot devised by the late L. L. Bean of Freeport, Maine, keeps more feet dry per square mile on Anderson Island than in any area so far from source of origin. All through February we sloshed about in Mr. Bean's boots. The mail brought a packet from a stranger—a pale blue lapel pin in the shape of a raindrop, inscribed with a testimonial, I LOVE RAIN, symbol of the I Love Rain Society. "To rainwash the world and keep Washington's image wet, to discourage crowds."

Of Mice and Shrews

Where meadow grass stayed flat, depressed by the weight of winter, beaten trails as intricate in engineering as Seattle freeways led to and from a maze of burrows, covered runways made by meadow voles (or hay mice), throughways mowed by chisel teeth and worn down by hurrying footsteps. Someone called them, aptly, "mouse dashes."

A volemouse never walks, he runs, or scurries. His life is brief and he must make the most of it, sustain himself and perpetuate his species. Under bending grass stems, moss-carpeted tunnels ran to seeps near the spring, branched, converged, and separated. Frenetic travelers left behind, as we do, small heaps of litter—gnawed stems, bits of root, chewed bark, messages that whispered, "Vole was here." Voles breed rapidly and prodigiously and must dash to gather food, to make new roads for expanding traffic. It is said that an acre of land may support a population as high as ten thousand meadow mice and that litters often consist of ten. Young sometimes breed at less than a month of age. Reproduction potential of a single pair may run 200 percent in four months' time. An exploding population must be fed, storage houses stocked, new nests and roads constructed for burgeoning families. The population bomb!

But mortality rate runs high. Enemies are legion—the owl by night, the hawk, the snake by day. Cats take their toll. Where the meadow rises to the woods our own and feral cats sit by the hour to watch the runways. A favorite hunting ground of our fat, neutered house cat, Lolly, is the rock wall where shrews run, often through tunnels made by mice. Genus *Sorex,* order *insectivore,* these small sad, mouse-like creatures, smallest of all mammals, will consume anything, flesh or vegetable, that gets in the way of their insatiable appetites. British call them "shrewmice." Ferocious, warlike by necessity, this tiny animal attacks and kills prey many times his weight, may make a meal of an unwary bird, even a fellow shrew. His keen nose comes to a point. His appetite, his need is torment.

I call Lolly inside when I catch him at the sport of shrew-hunting. He never eats his victim; he kills for fun, or practice. Dead or alive, the shrew is his plaything. A gland on the side of its velvet-soft body secretes a smelly fluid that repels the overfed cat. Even our mother cat brought live shrews to her kittens as toys or training props.

I pity this small animal that derives no pleasure, surely, from his frenetic life, passed in search of sustenance, bent on killing. Deprived of food, he would die in less than half a day. He devours his victim, skin, meat, bone, leaves not a trace. Weighing as little as one-third ounce, he is still a fearsome enemy. The pygmy shrew of northeast woods may weigh only one-quarter ounce. The water shrew, *Sorex palustris,* can walk or run on water. The life span of a shrew is mercifully brief, a year and a half at the most. He burns his candle at both ends. But in death he is free at last of his awful food requirement.

Woodpecker Territory

I had stopped one quiet morning to examine a brown polypore like a wooden-petaled morning glory when I heard a gentle, rhythmic tapping, curiously musical, a hollow tattoo, "b-t-t-t-t," pause, "b-t-t-t-t," silence. A dry madroña leaf dropped, and the busy sound began again, the unmistakable knocking of a downy woodpecker, the smallest member of the family *Picidae.*

After considerable search, I found him high on an alder bole, where he had made two neat strands of drillings, precise pits an inch apart, and was at work on a third, his tail clamped tightly against the bark for support, his head moving in a blurred, out-of-focus pattern. His scarlet nape stood out sharply above the white band on his black back. Rows of white French knots embroidered his black wing coverts. When I moved in order to see him better, he dodged quickly out of sight. But presently the drilling began again. Each time I moved, the performance was repeated. I tried to focus the glasses on him, but he kept the bole between us.

And so I left him to his artistry and wandered deeper into woodpecker territory. Live trees and dead snags, even stumps, were riddled with drillings, ranging from downy necklaces through the slightly wider pits left by his hairy cousin, to elongated vertical excavations with squared ends, the work of *Dryocopus pileatus,* the big western pileated known as "woodcock." Sometimes I hear them simultaneously or alternately, the gentle "tattattat," of the former, the loud persistent drumming of the latter, like the chattering of a machine gun or the compressed-air boring of a jackhammer.

The sight of the big, flashy cock-of-the-woods is always unexpected and often startling, a treat that makes any day a special one. I hear him often but I rarely see him. His hammer-shaped head is topped by a red cockade that gives him a bold, authoritative look. Southern mountain men call him "Lord God Woodpecker." His shyness makes sense; he may range in length to twenty inches, and he is all conspicuous black and white and red. His loud drum-

ming betrays his presence, and his flight is fast and undu-
lating, with sweeping wingbeats.

Having heard his hammering one morning, I located one
of these wary birds through glasses, near the pinnacle of a
tall fir snag nearly a quarter of a mile away. Whether he
was mining ants or grubs, to be lapped up with his long
probing tongue, or drilling a nest cavity, or simply trying to
attract a mate, I could not tell. He held to the typical woodpecker stance, spiny tail clamped against the spar to serve
as prop, zygodactyl feet planted firmly on the trunk. Only
his head moved, a blur of color.

As civilization advances his numbers diminish; he is said
to be on the brink of extinction. Early-day Indians used his
scarlet crest as ceremonial adornment, we crowd him out.
He must have space and solitude to stake out a nesting area
exclusively his own, a personal territory.

As I walked with a friend along a deserted Island road
one winter Sunday, we were stopped short by a pair of
pileated woodpeckers. Obviously unaware of us and intent
on their own affairs, they flew low across the road and literally threw themselves against the boles of two adjoining
trees. Their loud cackling "cuk-cuk-cuk" sounded hurried
and excited. We took them to be mates, as the one lacked
the red whisker stripe characteristic of the male bird.

At work in the garden above Higgins Cove on another
morning, I was startled by a rapidly moving shadow, as a
pileated swept past at eye level. Choosing to ignore me, although he was surely aware of my presence, he landed on
a stump less than twenty feet away and tore into the decaying mass with his swordlike bill. Tossing long strips of bark
aside, he fed on ants or grubs or whatever called the stump
home, and moved on at his leisure, while I stood motionless
and admiring.

The present western range of the pileated woodpecker is
small, this northwest corner plus a sparsely settled swatch
of British Columbia. The troubling thought occurs that for

those of us so fortunate as to share the Island with him he
may one day be a fading memory. To our children's children's children he may be nothing more than a hardly credible illustration in a natural history picture book.

Pilgrimage of Salamanders

The migratory movement of small native salamanders,
denizens of wet woods that seek fresh-water breeding
grounds, had begun in January before the snow, and the
pilgrimage continued through February and March and
well into April, gradually diminishing in numbers. During
the storm we had observed these little newts floundering
over and through the snowdrifts, instinct-driven toward the
swamp and lake waters. They emerged from the woods by
the hundreds, poured out in a red stream. Dark red, with
yellow underbellies, they resembled madroña twigs in motion. We drove slowly along the roads or turned aside to
avoid the mainstream of travel.

At first the migration was scattered and sporadic, but as
spring advanced the animals became more numerous. By
the last of February the procession was in full swing, a mass
movement. On the half-mile stretch of road from the chapel
to Rudolph Johnson's farm we counted hundreds. Road
ditches ran brim full of surface water after rain. How were
they to know they had not arrived at fresh-water breeding
grounds? Pointed by some internal direction finder, they
wriggled down the shoulder, entered the water, swam

across, and scrambled up the banks, to continue over stick and stone to their preordained destination.

In order to insure the safety of at least a few one heavy-traffic Sunday, my granddaughters and I walked the road to gather salamanders and carry them across. They felt clammy to the touch and wiggled and lashed their tails in an ungrateful manner. Because we liked to see them swim the ditches, we set them down on the opposite shoulder. They crossed with an agility born to water. Occasionally, to tease, we set one down facing the road. Not to be deceived, he would do a quick turnabout. We wished them all well and told them they were lucky to be Island salamanders. Roads in the vicinity of mainland lakes are literally strewn with corpses.

I cannot say when or whether these selfsame newts return to land life or what proportion of their lives is spent in water. We see them on the roads again in October and November, in lesser numbers, but moving in the opposite direction with the same determination. But whether they are homing travelers or newly hatched young, I do not know. I find them often in wet woods in various sizes, from three to five inches from nose to tip of tail.

Occasionally I see a lizard on the rock wall, but not often. Lizards have a dry and scaly skin in contrast to the moist, smooth hide of a salamander and do not thrive well in this cool climate. Typical lizards, an ancient reptile species, have five toes in contrast to salamanders' three or four to a foot. Our small red newts have *four* toes, and move in a sluggish, deliberate fashion as opposed to the former's swift-paced locomotion.

The Guthrie House

The road we call "the Guthrie Road" climbs a hill so steep and so soggy during winter months that county work

crews discontinued for a time the effort to cope with rivulets and gullies. Freshets found an easy course, deepened
and wore down to bedrock each rainy season, so that dis-
gruntled drivers left the road alone and took the long way
around.

During twenty years, I negotiated the hill on foot often.
At the top of the steep grade the road narrows and closes in
to become a tunnel roofed by interlocking arms of fir and
madroña and maple trees, a quiet aisle that seems, at mid-
way, to have no end and no beginning. One February afternoon I caught a glimpse of an albino doe in these woods, a
big spotted animal that resembled a yearling roan calf. She
may have gone down that fall before a hunter's gun, for I
never saw her but the once. With that coloring, in fall
woods, she would have made a prime target. But she may
have lived long enough to have produced albino offspring.
We hear occasional rumors of "white" deer seen in one
section or another of the Island.

Several worn deer trails cross the Guthrie Road to and
from Lake Florence, the shore of which runs approximately
parallel, although the lake remains unseen, hidden behind
a heavy stand of trees and undergrowth. On the lake side,
only one man-made path breaks the wood margin, a bending trail that leads to the privately owned dwelling we still
call "the Guthrie house," even though the man who gave
the place the name has been gone for years. The house is
used, now, by the current owners, the Peterson family. I
would like them to know both that I do not trespass there
any more and that I am grateful for earlier uninvited and
solitary visits.

During all of our first years here, the house stood unfinished, as it had for many years prior to that time, a fascinating skeleton surrounded by deep woods, unseen from the
road and hardly visible from the lakeshore. I was not the
sole intruder. The path from the house to the lake was
worn bare and I found cold ashes from campfires, carefully

contained, and human footprints in the mud, left by other trespassers.

The house was a retreat, a place to dream on. Neither finished nor lived in, it had no personality. It had aged alone. Beams and struts were weathered to a fine patina and the steep roof was blanketed with brown needles. Corners harbored mice and chipmunks. The wide, paneless windows framed panoramas of woods and lake. Cone-hung branches of a tall pine had invaded the upper story. Swallows nested on the ledges. Chickadees and siskins flew in and out, and wild band-tailed pigeons made hollow, ghostlike monosyllables along the rooftree.

We heard rumors about the place concerning who had built the skeleton and why it stood unfinished. I never learned the truth, nor wanted to. Whatever the builder's ethics, his concept was beyond his time. In an area of rural homes of a strictly utilitarian nature, the Guthrie house had an Old World charm. With a few turrets added it might well have served as castle and concealment for Sleeping Beauty.

Wing In

By the last of February we had begun to scan the sky for the vanguard of summer swallows. They must have come in the night. We awoke one morning to an unaccustomed chipping sound, and half a dozen violet-green swallows skimmed the air on long pointed wings, their green-purple (darker than violet) backs iridescent in the preview of sunlight. They settled for a moment's rest on the power line and were off again. The twittering sound came during resting periods; they flew in silence. Their swift gyrations made them seem more numerous than was actually the case. I could not help wondering what flying insects were in the cold air. The birds seemed ravenous. How far had they flown? How many hours, days, weeks? Had they come from Mexico, Central America, California? After a few days the air was netted with their crisscrossing flight, skimming, scooping, zooming out over water and back to land again. We never see migration here, as we did in Kansas, where we saw birds passing over in great flocks and patterns. Here, they seem to slip in overnight, or when our backs are turned.

As a child, I had never heard of "fly ways," routes taken by various species. The cries of wild geese flying north in spring and south in autumn were especially sweet music to our Dad, a self-taught naturalist, who drew word pictures for us of birds remembered from his own childhood in his native England. We watched the long V's out of sight and listened to their wild haunting harmony. We asked unanswerable questions. How was the leader chosen? Was the V formation designed for wind resistance? Did the geese change places according to some plan or pattern?

One night we watched a flight of pelicans, strange birds we had seen only in picture books, but unmistakable. Ducks, and sometimes geese, descended to the pasture ponds to rest and feed, and then were off again. But pelicans! The Arctic tern, we were told, flew ten thousand miles. More romantic and mysterious seemed the flight of smaller birds, that flew in silence, buffeted by winds. How did they know which way to go, and when the time had come to stop?

Blue-black barn swallows with long forked tails and soft tangerine breasts followed the violet-green. White-crowned sparrows with neat black-and-white striped berets appeared one morning on the feeder. I heard the red-winged blackbird before I saw him. His ringing "okalee . . ." came from the high crown of the cottonwood. His is a genuine spring song. The males, jet-black, with yellow margined, red epaulets come first, to stake out territory. We see them in the winter sometimes, but not around the house. Nor do

they nest here. They nest in the swamp or around the lakes.
I do not know why they come down here each spring. One
morning an answering call comes from the line of fir trees.
They call back and forth, a lovely sound, a special dispen-
sation.

Those who study flight patterns say the northward journey of most migrating species is made with greater speed.
The urge to preserve and to extend is stronger than the instinct to escape winter storms, to seek a ready food supply.

March

Vernal Equinox

Neither lamb nor lion, March came in with gentle rain. Wet purple finches sang in the still-bare willows, a low-pitched liquid warble, like water running over stones. The velvet raspberry crest of the males was burnished extra bright in advance of mating season. The sweet songs went on and on.

Alder seedlings along the shore bristled with upside-down bushtits. The lilting calls of the red-wings went on all day. A male and female came together to the feeder. Save for blackbird shape and swordlike bill, she was hardly recognizable as blackbird. Sooty brown in color, with broadly striped breast, she looked like an overgrown sparrow. It amuses me to think that the red-wing says his own scientific name, *"Agelaius,"* in four ringing syllables. At rest or feeding, only the yellow margin of his epaulet showed.

A male rufous hummingbird arrived one morning. He sat on a pine branch, turning and twisting his head to display his cold-fire gorget, a blinding flash of scarlet. But the show was wasted, the female had not come as yet. He flew off to investigate opening pendants on red-flower currant. Perhaps the nectar was not ready for he danced about on whirring wings, investigating the red reflector on the neighbor's mailbox, the taillights on the car, even a red glass bottle on the window sill.

Warned by *Audubon* magazine and other writings, we cut the syrup to one part sugar to nine parts water, a mixture he appeared to relish quite as well. After the female came, he settled down. Her feathers are a lovely green with iridescent patches to match her mate. They sat side by side on the wire perch, their long thread-like tongues intertwined in the syrup tube. Or so it looked to me.

We awoke one morning to a heavy hoarfrost. Long lacy strands of frost hung like lichen strands from every tree and bramble. Last year's rose hips were orange-scarlet beads on a flocked Yule tree. When sun emerged, the orchard burst into pseudo bloom, clouds of fringed white against a sky of delphinium blue. A black-capped chickadee hopped from branch to branch of the apricot as though his feet were cold. But then I saw him later stomping ice in the frozen birdbath. The day warmed slowly. Frost disappeared. It was spring again.

On clear nights the constellation Orion made a brilliant pattern in the sky. In the water, individual stars lay in place but faintly blurred, like objects out of focus in a photograph. Not the least of satisfactions that comes of living in the country is the fact that stars are infinitely brighter viewed from an earth unilluminated by electric power.

For days following the vernal equinox spring was evident only on the calendar. Sudden sharp rises and long quick plummets of mercury are almost unknown in this temperate climate, as we experienced them in the plains country. Weather reverted slowly to October or November. Rain beat in gusts against the windows. Water remained quiet close to shore; wind-rippled farther out, it took on an odd green color. White smoke arose from chimneys on the mainland and bent back to earth again. Horizon lines were curved and gentled by a blur of mist. Beyond the grayed point of Fox Island, water showed a soft mauve, the color of a dove's feathers.

Late one afternoon I surprised a little bird hawk, whether sharp-shinned or Cooper's I could not tell, lunching on a band-tailed pigeon. He stared up at me with sharp yellow eyes. Trapped temporarily by talons planted deeply in blue-gray feathers, he struggled for release. Free, he leapt into the air, gave a few quick wing beats, and glided off into a thick stand of conifers. The pigeon was still warm, but dead, and so I left it.

A haze of smoke from brush fires drifted through the wood and brought an acrid smell of burning rubber. Worn-out tires used in these heaps of rubbish smolder and smell for days sometimes. A downy woodpecker knocked softly, paused, and knocked again. But I could not find him among the new growth. In shady damp spots salmonberry buds were swollen. At this stage new growth is crisp and tender, and tastes like celery.

The Bird That Sings in the Night

Violet-green swallows fluttered indecisively about the nesting boxes. One tried in vain to enter a too-narrow hole in a ceramic birdhouse. He fluttered, headless, while his chosen mate waited. White-crowned sparrows filtered in from somewhere. These little gray-throated birds never come in numbers. *Striped* crown would seem a better name. The white stripe of the Puget Sound variety (*pugetensis*) begins at the bill, curves above the eye, and runs to the back of the crown. Black stripes alternate with white, giving the bird a tidy English housemaid look.

One year a pair of white-crowns built in the grass between protruding roots of a Spitzenberg apple tree. The top of the nest surprisingly enough was at ground level, as though the little builders had excavated and chosen basement living. Built on a foundation of fine roots, the cup was deep and softly lined. We marked the spot, to be avoided by the mower. The grass grew and bent over to make a natural roof.

Perhaps the white-crown was grateful. He (or she) sang a good deal, even late at night, keeping a distance from the nest. It sang unseen from the power wire or from the clothesline. Except for an occasional slur at the end, as though the bird had inadvertently struck a sour note, the song was remarkably sweet. In an area where there is a dearth of night singers, it was especially appealing. The song went on and on. I found a second nest that contained three speckled eggs of lovely turquoise blue low in a blackberry bush.

The white-crown is a domestic-seeming bird. He feeds on sheep sorrel that has already red-seeded on the lawn and at the base of the rock wall. A sour little plant, the most persistent I know, with the possible exception of ground ivy, this sorrel (*Rumex*) has an affinity for old sawdust mulch, in which it springs up and spreads like wildfire.

As children, we gave the name of sheep sorrel to quite another plant, "wood sorrel," an oxalis with trifoliolate, cloverlike, or "shamrock" leaves and an acid taste. Wood sorrel, as the name suggests, grows in the woods here and has pink blossoms. The bloom of sheep sorrel is greenish, seed heads an attractive red. A second wood sorrel, *Oxalis suksdorfii,* with yellow blossoms, seeks open spaces, has tiny red-bronze leaves.

Pest though it is, sheep sorrel is an interesting plant, of ancient lineage. Lower leaves are hastate, shaped like little spears. The word comes from the Latin *hastatus,* from *hasta,* meaning spear. Some gardeners call it "redweed," others, "sourweed." Pliny wrote in the first century, "When it [sheep sorrel] has taken root it will last forever and can never be extirpated from the soil." Truer words were never written. Fifteen centuries later, Englishman John Evelyn wrote that this everlasting sorrel "sharpens the appetite, cools the liver and strengthens the heart . . . and in the making of salats imparts a grateful quickness to the rest as supplying the want of oranges and lemons."

The Great Blues

One morning as I passed along the road that skirts Oro Bay two great blue herons landed on the high bough of a fir tree. Flying or feeding, these big lean birds with six-foot wingspread show little color, only a drab gray-blue. Against the tender green of spring fir growth, they looked like enormous blue flowers with drooping petals.

No bird is more impressive. In bays and coves, at ebb tide, they stand tall and still and composed, dignified grandfathers. Or they walk slowly with heads hunched, like old men deep in thoughts of past adventures. They take off

clumsily, generally in silence, wide wings lifted. Once airborne, their thin whitish heads are carried well back. Head
and neck form the letter **S**. Wings hang downward. Long
legs trail like bent sticks. I cannot distinguish male from
female.

   When they do give voice, they emit harsh, startling
squawks. I first heard the sound from the wooded trail
above Higgins Cove. I stopped, frozen. The sound came
again. And then the owner of the voice appeared. He swept
up the gulch like a big blue kite, motorized. The cruising
speed of a great blue has been clocked at twenty miles per
hour, in contrast to the forty miles per hour credited to a
mallard. Year-around Islanders, the blues are geared down
to Island pace. Nesting sites, so far, are ample, food (fish
and frogs and other aquatic life) abundant.

One year a great blue heron discovered a set of bait boxes, anchored by fishermen below low-tide line off New Amsterdam Bay, and settled there. He remained for days. When the bait boat arrived with a fresh supply, he arose in a leisurely fashion and flapped across to the shore. As soon as the boat was gone, he returned to select his meal at will from among the lively herring. As do the harbor seals, herons nest unmolested on Gertrude Island off Mc-Neil and fish in Still Harbor.

They nest on Anderson, too. For several years a pair of great blues has nested in tall firs on the bank high above Higgins Cove. One morning I watched a peculiar drama being played on a bare limb of a half-dead hemlock. One (the female, perhaps) sat quietly near the tree bole. The other stalked back and forth, back and forth, four feet tall, like a husband delivering a lecture. I chose to think he looked wrought up, but perhaps he was only showing off his plumage.

A guest at the cove came across an even more dramatic sight. Down along the shore, he said, two of these birds appeared to be engaged in battle. They ran at each other, towering and ferocious, wings spread wide and sword-sharp bills pointed directly at each other. A third heron stood nearby and took no part, as though quietly awaiting the outcome of the skirmish. Unfortunately, the guest's appearance broke up the contest before the matter was decided.

One hulking specimen I took to be a juvenile hung around the cove near the nesting site all summer. His favorite perches were a fir above the water and a broadleaf maple thick with foliage. When I walked along the beach I tried to prepare myself for the nerve-assaulting jolt by locating him before he took flight. But he played a game of hide-and-seek and invariably flushed with jarring squawks from an unexpected quarter.

King of Fishermen

I am always reluctant to leave the cove. So much goes on there, especially in spring. The raffish little belted kingfisher pays scant attention to my comings and goings. I show up so frequently that he can ill afford to waste his time in hiding. I like to think he has come to trust me.

He is another that is frequently unseen until he makes his sudden dive at flow tide when the cove is full. He bolts headlong from a jutting limb, hovers and takes his catch, and then slants upward to the opposite side. If his victim gives him trouble, he beats its head against the perch to stop its struggles. Even when the cove is empty or only beginning to fill, he may chatter from one side to the other without apparent reason.

Some say the sound is a ruse intended to confuse his potential victim. He pretends to be terrifying, and I suppose he is to some hapless herring. To me he is the clown of the cove. His bushy crested head is too big for his body.

His wings beat hard and fast. His rattle seems too loud for his size. His syndactyl feet are well adapted for his work, two toes webbed together for a portion of their length. His bill is sword shape. The cones in his retina contain oil droplets that act as color filters, as a camera is equipped to counteract brightness and provide contrast.

Except during breeding season he seems to be a loner at the cove. The nest is constructed deep in a clay bank, or at the end of an excavation in diatomaceous earth. Sometimes he appropriates a burrow excavated by another species. For a little while during nesting season he enjoys considerable company. His mate boasts a rusty band below the blue belt. Whether she comes to him or he leaves the cove to seek her out I have no notion. For a time after hatching, the off-spring are present. The cove is filled with kingfishers, div-ing, crossing, rattling. And then he is alone again.

I always wonder where the others go. I see a solitary kingfisher, or perhaps a pair, on Oro Bay or on New Am-sterdam. I suppose they must fish all the coves and inlets, as well as lakes and swamp. Occasionally one comes to open shore here on Yoman Point, where alder and wild cherry crowd the high bank. He takes up a position on one of these and works for a time, then moves down the shore toward the ferry slip. With a limited number of lagoons, coves, sloughs, and inlets, I am puzzled as to where all his progeny find waterways for solo fishing. Perhaps only ours maintains his status as a perennial bachelor.

Forward, March

The first wildflowers to come into bloom, if you except the shrubs oso-berry and wild red-flower currant, are the big lavender or pinkish heads of sweet-scented coltsfoot, or butterbur, that grow along damp banks and roadsides. The loose balls of flowers appear on naked scaly stems well in advance of lobed maple-like leaves, and a little way apart. During my first spring in the Northwest I failed to associate flower and leaf, and took the plant to be leafless, or like the crocus we call "naked lady lily" that flowers alone after the leaves have died away.

Coltsfoot, a composite whose scientific name is *Petasites,* points up the need for scientific names. In England, indeed in eastern portions of this country, the name of coltsfoot is given to quite a different flower, *Tussilago farfara,* a *Compositae* whose leaves, too, put in a tardy appearance. Both plants have a reputation for curing coughs. Hereabouts, Indians cooked and ate leaves and young stems. Reduced to ashes, they are said to provide a reasonable substitute for salt.

On a shelf formed by a bank slide at the north end of the island, a drift of coltsfoot spreads farther each successive year. Fragrant blooms stand among the twisted roots of undermined trees in early March. In a month they will have gone to seed. Even the loose seedballs resemble flowers. The lobed long-stemmed leaves, white-woolly and a foot across, follow the flowers and stand a little way apart.

Of spring shrubs, oso-berry is among the first to bloom. Some call it Indian plum, bird cherry, or skunk bush. Often as early as February nodding flower pendants in the shape of tiny white trumpets dangle on red toothpick stems below clusters of small upstanding leaves. The shrub has a whimsical fringed look. Because flowers come too early to be fertilized by bees, nature has endowed them with a strong smell (some say skunk, some say watermelon) to attract cruising flies. The flowers open so slowly and so sporadically and remain in bloom for such a long time that bees have come before blossoms are completely gone

And now comes the skunk cabbage, which deserves a better name than either "skunk" or "cabbage." The first green spears of leaves thrust up in swamp and marsh and bog, even before oso-berry comes to bloom. By the last of

March yellow spathes and spadices lighten low wet woods like shielded candles. The club-shaped spadix embraced by a single yellow "petal" carries small green flowers. On either side pale green leaves stand three feet or more in length in rich mucky places. The effect of a patch of skunk cabbage in a dark bog is that of a vast room illuminated by hundreds of pale lemon-colored flames; you can almost see them flicker.

Skunk cabbage is an arum, as are calla lily and philodendron. Unless the plant is crushed, the sweet civet odor is only mildly apparent and not offensive. I have stood entranced in the center of a drift of nearly half an acre of these and caught no scent at all. Far more apparent is the skunk odor given off by Jacob's ladder, a *Polemonium* that bears the name of "skunkleaf." Having seated myself one day to enjoy a sandwich in the midst of a patch of blue Jacob's ladder, I was suddenly engulfed by the smell. Believing that I had stumbled onto a skunk's territory, I beat a cautious retreat. I did not know the lovely, soft-blue flowers of this "skunkleaf" then.

Northwest Indian folklore contains a charming story about skunk cabbage, whose thick rootstock is said in earlier times to have saved certain of their ancestors from starvation "before Salmon came." Arriving on the scene and being apprised of this fact, Salmon gave to this plant an elkskin blanket (the yellow, oblong, platter-shaped spathe leaf), placed a club (the spadix) in Skunk Cabbage's hands, and gave him a place of honor beside the stream up which Salmon came to feed his people.

Of late years skunk cabbage has crept farther and farther from the swamp to fill the spreading bog along Otso Point Road, and has spread up the shoulder to stand in a line even in the median in the low seeps. Said to be related to taro, used as a food by people of the Pacific Islands, the plant contains crystals of calcium oxalate in all parts. Cooking removes the sting. Occasionally in midsummer after the big leaves have collapsed and the spathe has fallen away, I find clumps of red berries ripened on the spadix. But these are quickly gone, whether eaten by birds or by rodents I do not know.

By the last of March wild red-flower currant, no more than five or six feet in height, was in full blossom, and rufous hummingbirds had descended in numbers. Wherever woods are open—along shaded roadsides and bordering cleared sites for earlier portable sawmills—this crooked little nondescript shrub dripped with bright racemes that varied from deep pink to crimson. In the open the bush grows taller, to nine feet or better. For as long as I have used the winding trail that terminates at the sandspit on Higgins Cove a wild red currant has stood beside the path. March through April and sometimes well into May, until the last of the aromatic flowers is gone, the shrub serves as smorgasbord for touch-and-go hummingbirds.

March brings too much too fast. The narrow trail that follows the creek up the gulch from the old ram to the settling barrel and beyond has remained for the most part unused since the ram that lifted the water to the house ceased to function. The lift seemed a kind of natural miracle, as did the lift of water by the force of wind on windmill blades in the Southwest, and so I regret the ram's retirement. It occurs to me sometimes that we have gone too far in our dependence upon manufactured power. I come away puzzled from meetings of our own cooperative, where the program embraces predictions of power shortages and at the same session urges the consumption of *more* power in the interest of reduced rates.

When we depended on the ram we kept the trail open so that we could periodically clean the screen that covered the settling barrel and clear the spring of fallen leaves. Cleaning the spring provided a fine excuse for a junket. To reach the spring, half-way up the slope on the opposite side of the gulch, it was necessary to wend one's way along a narrow path between banks of sword fern and maidenhair and marching lines of creek-side blackcap and salmonberry, cross the creek on a moss-covered spanning log, and follow the carrying pipe to the spot where a stream of clear cold water descended through another system of filter screens of various dimensions, collecting basins for sand and soil from above and for a wide variety of needles and leaves.

The spring was not on the Higgins place, though the Higgins house by way of the ram was the only dwelling the source supplied. When we first came by the place this fact worried us a bit because of the intricate maze of legal gobbledygook that goes by the term of "water rights." Oscar Johnson, the owner of the spring, accorded us a surprised look.

"Well, you're welcome to the water. Nobody *else* uses it, and there's plenty and to spare."

Water rights, he meant to say, like corner stakes and surveys, like deeds to the natural area around the lakes, were simply unimportant here. Water, firewood, leaf mold, berries, greens, and Christmas trees were for whoever had need of them. This give and take, we came to learn, made up in no small part the charm and pleasure of Island living. I recall a day when I asked permission of Oscar's brother Rudolph to look for meadow mushrooms in the farm pasture. Rudolph, too, appeared surprised. "You sure you know which ones are toadstools?" he asked me.

With so much to be seen along the path that crossed the creek and ascended the slippery steep side of the gulch to the spring, I made slow progress. Where trees had gone down, admitting sunlight, green lupine seedlings, silvery thistle rosettes, diminutive foxglove leaves, and mats of furry alumroot had all shouldered their way by late March through the covering mulch of last year's detritus. The air was redolent of leaf mold. Blackcap, a wild black raspberry with recurved thorns and sharp-pointed leaflets, sprawled across the pathway, in competition with its thornless cousin thimbleberry. Above the ram the creek sang through a hollow log that lay at right angles beneath a man-made dam of moss-clothed logs.

Why this barricade was built here, or when, I have never heard. The logs are half returned to earth, covered over by licorice ferns with thin tapered fronds lobed to midrib, thick with round brown sori. Stems and rootstocks have a strong licorice flavor.

Beside the settling barrel, overflowing now into the creek, dark red salamanders moved about among wet leaves. Heart-shaped leaves of wild ginger spread a mat on the shaded slope and sent up a spicy smell from hairy stems. Rooted at the nodes, the stems taste like gingersnaps.

Deer had crossed from the open orchard, and raccoons had left a network of tracks. Thimbleberry and madroña shoots were browsed clean. Even new leaves on bitter cherry had been tasted. Stopped short by a spider's web hung like a tollgate across the path, I stopped to admire the architecture, three delicate silver guy threads that held in place a plate-sized doily of finest gossamer. The builder was not in sight, but two coarsely woven triangular bags off to one side appeared to be occupied, whether by family or by snared victims.

In the hope that the master (or mistress) of the manse might put in an appearance, I sat down to wait. An intruder such as I has only to sit still in the gulch for a little time, and life resumes its regular tempo. A band-tailed pigeon homed in. He landed heavily, for he is a big bird, swayed for a moment on a rocking bough of hemlock, and moved to a more secure position in a broadleaf maple. I sat motionless. He was so close I could see the soft rose-gray of his breast feathers and head blending into slate blue, the white neck crescent and dove-gray tail feathers, like a banded fan. When I made an involuntary movement to ease cramped muscles, he was off and in seconds was lost among the trees.

In order to avoid disturbing the spider's web, I hacked a path through thimbleberry and crossed the creek. In a moss-lined pocket of the log bridge, a baby wood slug lay curled beneath a mushroom umbrella. When I touched him with a finger he stiffened and hardened, a defensive tactic.

The screens were plugged tight with sand and leaves, but the water was as clear, cold, and delicious as I remembered it to be. I left the spring and continued the climb to the road above. All through the open woods new growth was shouldering its way up through the deep mulch of fallen leaves. My feet sank in leaf mold. The machete, plunged into velvet-soft soil, went all the way to the hilt.

As I stepped into the road a doe and last year's fawn melted from sight. I walked along the shoulder, searching among the big stones rolled over by the county grader for the fossil-studded rock Nella Higgins had told me about. We had searched together one morning but had not found it. Having found a small rock near the spot another day, with embedded prints of ancient cockle and butter clam, I could only conclude that the boulder size she described had been buried or broken.

Of Cockles and Chiton and Triton

On a gray March day the beach seems seasonless. But here, too, is a stir of creativity. A rich salt smell comes from the empty cove. From the wet rocks spurt spasmodic fountains. I find exposed masses of bright yellow gelatinous capsules, snail eggs arranged in rows, like beaded doilies. I have watched the snail at work. He makes his slow-paced rounds as deftly as does a woman with a crochet hook. The eggs do not all hatch at once. Older larvae consume younger. Finally, only a few survive. Hundreds perish that one may live, survival not of the fittest but of the earliest.

During twenty years of searching at extreme low tides,

I have found only two *entire* shells of this Oregon triton. The shell is as lovely, as delicate, with its beaded, axial riblets, as Belleek porcelain. Shaped like a trumpet, the shell is a clear translucent white under the bristled covering that protects the animal from boring enemies. In tropical waters tritons grow to a length of eighteen inches, and the natives drill holes into the sides of the spires to convert them into musical instruments with a cornet sound. The operculum that closes the aperture once the animal has withdrawn is a thin oval sheet of amber.

I find bits and pieces of the fragile latticework of the skeleton shell, beaten and grated to fragments by rolling water on rocky beaches. I have never found one alive. I picked up a handsome triton once, only to discover that a hermit crab had taken up residence and declined to be ejected.

At a minus-three tide, beaches that fan out from creeks and freshets harbor layers of lives that vary from the highly salt-tolerant to those that require a merely brackish environment. A single boulder only occasionally exposed in its entirety supports a community ranging from barnacles through blue mussels, anemones, pile worms, snails, limpets, chitons, perhaps a starfish or two, all in close association. In greatest profusion, if you discount the barnacles, are the thin-shelled mussels that occur in masses, held together by byssal threads.

Smaller and sturdier snails than tritons, purple, brown, orange, striped, lie among the pebbles or cling to rocks, their horny opercula closed, awaiting flow tide. Stout doors of barnacle castles, too, remain closed. I have heard that people with acute hearing can detect the click of these doors closing. Beach hoppers (not "fleas" but amphipods) arise before me as I walk. Limpets, like tiny Oriental hats, cling to stones, to abandoned shells and shells of living animals, and to each other.

Among the strangest in this universe of the fantastic is

the giant chiton. I come across him fairly often on a sandy beach at low tide. He resembles an old boot sole. No shell is visible. The eight thin white dorsal plates that resemble bone china butterflies lie buried in his flesh. I found these on the beach for years before I associated them with their lumpy, unprepossessing owner.

Likewise puzzling were the sand collars of moon snails strewn along the beach at low tide. I took them to be some kind of peculiar rubber gasket, lost off ships perhaps. Formed around the female shell as the eggs are deposited, these gelatinous masses containing thousands of eggs are left on the beach to dry. Once dry and brittle, they break up. Larvae hatch and swim about until they become adults with shells of their own.

On sandy beaches I find numerous moon snails. Trails terminate in small mounds that barely conceal the animal. The fleshy "hoof" all but engulfs the shell. Somewhere in that moist flesh lies a hapless clam, smothered or drilled through. Taken up, the moon snail ejects a steady stream of water, as you would wring out a mop, becomes smaller and smaller. Having tucked his bulk, finally, into his shell, he closes his only door, a snug-fitting, horny operculum, an amazing transformation.

Life goes on here as in our own world, beginning and ending, thrifty and prodigal, cruel and kind. Once inside his shell, the moon snail is an object of beauty. The beauty of the ugly chiton lies *inside*. The tide has reached its ebb. A time of slack prevails. The flow commences. Salt water curls around the spit, to be met by fresh. How many times has this marriage been repeated? How much longer will the little nameless stream rise and run to meet the waters of the Sound that extend to merge with the waters of the Strait that dilute the salt of the Pacific Ocean? When is influence lost beyond recounting?

April

Honestie

March ended on a note of gentle wind and warmth, and April began. We turned a page on the calendar and there was the magic month, the month of bud and blossom. Rosettes of honestie plant appeared along the east shore among fireweed and bracken. Each year the plant spreads farther. Seeds blow and sprout. Sprouts grow and bloom and reach fulfillment.

In an effort to trace the plant's history I opened a book

entitled *Old Fashioned Gardens* by Alice Morse Earle.*
Here was honestie under a variety of names, all of them
intriguing and descriptive, none of them scientific. Not
given to romanticism, *Encyclopædia Britannica* lists the
plant as *Lunaria annua* of the family *Cruciferae,* or mustard, to which are assigned draba, rock cress, Whitlow
grass, with oval flattened seed pods. The *Wise Garden Encyclopedia* spells the name "honesty."

The seed pods give the plant its names as well as its
beauty. Mrs. Earle calls it satin flower, or white satin. In
Elizabethan days the plant was pricksong, from the shape
of the seeds, like notes of music. The French call them *im-
mortelles* because of their "everlasting" quality. Like Mrs.
Earle, I prefer the name honestie or money-in-both-pockets.

How honestie came to grow so thick here I have no notion. Perhaps it was planted in a dooryard by some early
settler's wife and made its way around. It is as much a
wildflower now as is foxglove, the delicate pink blossoms
of Himalaya blackberry, or the bright orange cones of California poppy. What is wild? Most plants are wild in some
variety somewhere.

The pinkish purple flower of honestie is unspectacular.
Individual blossoms are too massed together. But the seed
valves are delightful, coin-shaped pockets of translucent
tissue-thin "paper" through which the seeds are visible.
Stalks were used long ago as winter bouquets, along with
yarrow, everlasting, teasel, strawflower, and the burnt-
orange seed pods of Montbretia. In 1760 Boston house-
wives carried on small respectable home enterprises in seeds,
a form of Women's Lib. One of these ladies included
honestie with a note of explanation, "To be sold in small
parcels that everyone may have a little."

Wherever the plant originated, however it came to American shores, by 1901 it had spread so freely, especially in
northern Connecticut, that it grew wild by the waysides.

* New York and London: Macmillan, 1901.

The story goes that a New England village "addlepate" by the name of Elmer who made his way by rush-seating chairs and weaving baskets lived in an old barn and associated with the village children. Taking his cue from the children, who used the pods of honestie as play money, Elmer gathered and stored. If he were in need he simply proffered the seeds at the village store, where they were accepted as collateral by the kind-hearted storekeeper. Or he presented the coin-shaped seeds to villagers, who fed and clothed him in return, not wishing Elmer to feel that he was an object of charity. Having heard Elmer boast of his hoard of "silver," two rascals searched his place. When they found only jars of seeds, the burglars threw the jars outside and beat Elmer so severely that he died of his wounds.

Carried away and scattered by the wind, the seeds sprouted throughout the countryside. The following summer honestie bloomed so lavishly among daisies over the hills surrounding the town that people came from miles around to marvel at the beauty of the place and to ponder over the mixture of evil and charity in men's hearts, as well.

The Two Sisters

On an April Sunday in the year 1854 an adventurous young man named Michael Luark made his way slowly among fallen trees and dense underbrush up a two-hundred-foot bluff on Anderson Island, attracted (we may conjecture) by the ax blows of a pileated woodpecker on some old spar or snag.

Breaking into the open, he was surprised to find himself on the shore of a mirror-clear lake. The sight of this body of still, sparkling water so high above the Sound filled him with excitement. Although the day was warm for April, the water was ice cold. Puzzled as to its origin, he set out to pace the shore line in an effort to find the source and in an attempt to gauge the length and breadth of the jewel-like body of water.

The young man met hard going. Along the water's edge a miniature forest of hardhack topped by brown husk steeples hampered his footsteps. In places, because March had been a rainy month, his feet sank half-way to the tops of his stout logging boots. Branches of fir, cedar, hemlock, and the broadleaf evergreen madroña, which he knew as "laurel," softened the shore line and gave back reflections from the sunlit water.

Making his way along the low bank, counting his foot-steps as he went, Luark perceived that the lakeshore bent to the north and then straightened to run west by east. As he looked down the length of the body of water from the end, marveling at its sparkling beauty, he estimated the lake to be approximately one and one-half miles by about eighty rods, a computation he found later to be accurate enough. Except at the extreme ends, the breadth appeared to show little variance.

Because of the density of growth and because he was frequently distracted by the "sporting" of fish and by large ducks swimming about, Luark made slow progress. When he had reached marshy ground after negotiating about half the length along the south shore, he came unexpectedly upon a small stream that flowed *away* from the lake. An outlet!

Curious as to where the brook might lead, he turned to follow its course. After a few steps he saw through the not yet completely leafed deciduous foliage that another body of water lay to the south. A dozen or more additional steps brought him to the edge of a second lake, only a little lower than the first. Standing on the shore at the narrow end, he looked across a shallow filled with cat-tails and pond lilies down a gradually widening stretch to a broad expanse as mirror-like as the first had been.

When he had made his way with difficulty to the far shore of the second lake he found that this one, too, was provided with a small outlet that descended gently for a little way and then fell into a deep gully, to reach salt water in about eighty rods, with a fall of approximately two hundred feet in this distance. From the top of the bluff at the edge of the gully, Luark cast a stone and heard it splash after an interval into the waters of Puget Sound.

Looking across the channel toward Cormorant Passage, he saw that the southwest point of Gove's Island (now Ketron) lay in his direct line of vision and that all of the mainland to the east, including snow-blanketed Mount Rainier and the foothills of the Cascade Mountains, were in magnificent view. Seeing no signs of man's influence as he made his way back through fern, huckleberry, salal, and other tall brush, deciduous as well as evergreen, to his temporary shelter in the logging camp, young Luark concluded that he had discovered the lakes. The thought pleased him.

That evening he recorded the supposed discovery in his diary, kept faithfully during his entire sojourn in the Northwest Territory, and named the lakes "The Twin Sisters." He had seen many lakes during his journey from his claim on the Cowlitz River in search of work, but he had seen nothing to compare with these high, secluded, hidden bodies of clear cold water without visible inlet. Lost in dense concealing growth, on an uninhabited island marked by only a few temporary logging camps, the area looked to be a haven for wildlife. "The island would make a fine rich man's residence," he concluded, perhaps wistfully. But then, with a "those-grapes-are-sour" flourish, he dismissed all of the land north of the Cowlitz as "poor and unproductive."

Nearly a score of Aprils passed before the Island began

to settle, and more than an additional decade became history before any portion of the wooded shores of either lake was inhabited by man. Except for a small clearing between the two, the area around both lakes remained heavily wooded, a natural habitat for wildlife. From March to October, violet-green swallows dipped and dived in the clean air and cast moving reflections. Water striders drew rapid patterns on the quiet surface. Frogs sang or remained silent. Red-winged blackbirds nested among the cat-tails and shrilled the throaty "okalee's" that announced their territorial boundaries. During winter and spring migrations ducks and geese stopped to rest.

In nearby woods cavity-dwelling birds, from chickadee to pileated woodpecker, built in dead snags. Deer came and went undisturbed, weaving beaten paths through the underbrush, and muskrats played along the banks. Even man's first coming made little impact. Charles Alward and John Dahl filed homestead claims. The higher of the lakes was named Lake Florence, for Florence Alward. No one had heard of Michael Luark and his remarkable discovery. The second lake was named, years later, for Josephine Hopkins, the wife of a later owner.

The sound of the ax and the crosscut were added to the hammering of the big woodpeckers and the drilling of the downy. On the lakes an occasional splash of a dipping oar mingled with the deep harsh croaks of the great blue heron and the rattle of the belted kingfisher, the lonely crying of soaring seagulls and the cawing of crows in flight.

After the Alwards and the Dahls had gone, the area belonged (as did the strip of woods that bordered Lake Florence on the north) to everyone and to no one. No matter who held the deeds, the deeply wooded as well as the burned-over land was open range for fishing, wood-cutting, brush- and berry- and mushroom-gathering. No road worthy of the name ran beyond the cemetery to the high-bank east shore. But negotiable trails meandered among second-growth fir and opportunist alder, turning and twisting to avoid stumps and snags, as the first roads built across the Island had done. Bald eagles nested on the bluff, coming and going across the channel.

As we saw how it was after a while, we made so bold as to cut our own Yule trees there, and took occasional bark mulch and leaf mold from decaying logs and stumps near the lakeshore. Most of my own trespassing was done in early morning when true wild blackberries or evergreen huckleberries had ripened in open spaces. Bearing briars of the *Rubus macropetalus* ran along the ground to a length of ten or twelve feet among knee-high alder and tall dead spars in strange shapes, charred reminders of that which had been living heartwood. Firs had come up among the alders, and in early spring the place was alive with bird song and bright with dangling pendants of wild red currant and oso-berry. On foggy mornings deer drifted across the narrow roads and vanished without a sound among the thick undergrowth.

Johnson's Landing

One afternoon the last of the stern-wheelers, operated now by the Army Corps of Engineers and soon to be retired, nosed up the slot between Anderson and McNeil islands. Long before she came into view, even before she had passed the stake light and bell on Eagle Reef, we could hear the steady liquid rhythm of the wheel, the musical churning the Johnson children described as an "over and over sound."

The stern-wheeler is a curiosity now, a has-been kept in running condition more or less for old time's sake. To the Islanders who remember when both stern- and side-wheelers stopped at the landing, she is a conversation piece and evokes strong nostalgia. The three surviving Johnson children—Bessie, Ben, and Otto—still live on the Island. They will all be sorry to see her go.

As this last of the steamboats came into view, pushing a barge load of snags and deadheads taken from the water, we could see the silver cascade over the wheel. Passing the federal penitentiary on McNeil, she gave a hoarse salute that bounced an echo off the trees and buildings.

Rosamond Ferrari, now of California but then of Vashon Island, remembers watching both side- and stern-wheelers pass Vashon shores en route "Down and Up Sound." "Surely," she recalled with a laugh, "you called the stern-wheelers 'wet asses'?" Bessie, eighty-four, does not remember this. Bessie has written of her own memories in her book *Island Memoir*.* "During the years 1882 until about 1905, the Johnson Woodyard was a beehive of activity. The stern wheelers *Capital City, City of Aberdeen, State of Washington, Greyhound,* and others landed regularly at Johnson's Landing (as the woodyard became known) for wood and water. . . . We children never tired of watching those three-story steamers come in to the landing, guided skillfully by the captain from his elevated post."

Each year around the first of April I like to pay a visit to the ruins of Johnson's Landing. The landing is little more than a place name, now, on the map of Anderson Island Quadrangle published by the Army Corps of Engineers, as are the "towns" Yoman and Vega, once post-office sites for Island residents. The logs that made up the cabin where Bengt and Anna Johnson lived have been carefully numbered and hauled to Otso Point to be reassembled. The blackened stone chimney still stands on the original site close by the shambles of a building once known as "the teamsters' cabin."

During the months of April, May, and June, life triumphant renews itself on the bank above the landing and back around the shards of the barn that housed the Johnson

* Puyallup, Wash.: The Valley Press, 1969.

horses. In the tall grass, green and white snowdrops with delicate petal tracings open sleepy bells among yellow and purple crocus planted by Anna Johnson; and hop vines, seeded not for beauty but for bread, seek support among the ruins. Pear trees bloom and bear in the old orchard, and the teamsters' cabin is all but smothered by a rambler rose.

Spring Fever

For three days rain fell steadily without a break in the low gray clouds. Overhead, planes mumbled out of sight, passenger planes from Seattle-Tacoma Airport and from Tacoma Industrial, private planes, training planes from McChord Air Force Base, reminders that we are a part of the world beyond Island shores. When two or three weeks pass without my having crossed the channel, I find myself reluctant to make the break. In love with tranquillity, I find no compelling reason.

I can keep in touch with mainland friends by daily mail, Star Route. Of recent years we can communicate by underwater telephone cable. We have radio and television, a daily paper. I may walk a mile or two on an open road, or drive the length of the Island, without meeting a pedestrian or an automobile.

Once I drive off the ferry onto the mainland, I am aware of obligations, conscious that I need a haircut, uncomfortable in unaccustomed "dress-up" clothing. I am bothered by traffic and parking problems, the sight of strange faces, the push of people, markets stocked with thirty brands of laundry detergents and as many varieties of breakfast cereals, a plethora of margarines, salad dressings, canned goods, and beverages. I read labels, consider ingredients, compute weights and prices, dally and delay decisions, grow impatient with surfeit, and return to the Island to do the bulk of my shopping at Lyle Carlson's store on Oro Bay.

Each year sees more visitors to the Island. Bright, warm week ends bring cars and cycles and hikers in increasing numbers. Morning and early afternoon ferries on Saturdays and Sundays disgorge more strange foot passengers and more unfamiliar cars than we formerly saw here in a year's time. Yet we still mark the fact that within fifteen minutes the roads may be free of cars. They have vanished into the woods or down some wooded trail to a private beach. In all probability they will not be seen again until they filter out onto the roads to line up for the outbound sailing.

This influx, in a populous area, is not surprising. I have been accused, at least once, of a reluctance to share the satisfaction, the charm of Island living. This is not the case. But let me dream. Were I to be given an opportunity I would set a population limit, so that each might enjoy space and solitude, unspoiled woods, uncrowded roads, and a chance to become a part of a community sufficiently unpopulous that he would be (as we are privileged to be) on a first-name basis with every other individual Islander.

April was a month of wind and sun and cloud, a time alive with the songs and the feverish building of returned birds. Here on the shore the wind tasted and smelled of iodine and salt. In the woods the fragrance of leafmold mingled with the heady aroma of spring growth. Sunlight struck more often through the trees, lighted the dappled gray of alder and hazel, the clean mahogany boles of madroña from which thin skinlike bark rolled back in patches to reveal a tender chartreuse. As the month wore on, the cloud mantle was lifted more frequently from the face of Mount Rainier and the outlines of the crater showed plainly against a delft-blue sky. Shower and sun took turns. A single day might see three, four, or half-a-dozen rainbows.

Gathering debris of decaying logs to use as mulch in the

garden or collecting moss for the hanging baskets, I wandered deeper into the woods. Any excuse at all would do. Smells, sights, and sounds beckoned. Blankets of yellow-green moss clothed logs, stumps, and boulders. How had these big stones come into the forest? They seemed out of place. Some mosses were frosted with lidded capsules in red and vermillion. Queer sooty fungi, like tiny upraised fingers, crumbled at a touch.

One log supported a miniature garden—lady and licorice fern, red huckleberry seedlings with delicate green angled stems, star flower and vanilla leaf, wild blackberry and wild rose, inch-tall fir, cedar, and hemlock trees. A boulder shrouded with moss was starred with trailing yellow violets and pink massed bloom of Siberian miner's lettuce. Fir blocks recently sawed scented the air with the clean smell of live sap.

In a sheltered spot, flowers of Oregon grape were bright gold among spiny holly-shaped leaves. Patches of stinging nettle carpeted open spaces. At this stage, nettle is edible, as are the still-sleeping, circinate fronds of bracken fern.

Rufous hummingbirds increased in numbers. Males fought fiercely, rising high in the air to strike at each other, swiveling to keep their sword bills pointed toward their adversaries. They threatened, hovered, stabbed, retreated, hissed, shifted gears, and moved out of range to return to the energy-restoring syrup. Males took turns gyrating, solo, before a small green inattentive female. They postured and posed, displaying gorgets like coals of fire, moved, rested, and returned to battle. It is said that a resting hummingbird breathes 250 times per minute, to man's 16. A hummer's stout heart makes up one-fifth of its few ounces of body weight. In its constant need it is cousin to the shrew and must keep up a never-ending quest for food. A holiday means death.

Crisp white bracts of Pacific dogwood, like fresh, starched

doilies, appeared overnight. A symmetrical, deciduous tree, with blackish or gray-brown bark, the dogwood is distinguished at any season. In April it is a spectacular sight against the new light-green growth of conifers. Parallel veins run lengthwise on the leaves. Small greenish flowers are surrounded by broad white sepals that make up the "bloom."

An intriguing member of the same family is the little dwarf cornel, *Cornus canadensis,* pigeonberry or bunchberry, that stands no more than a few inches tall, a modest replica with white, petal-like bracts. Greenish-lavender flowers produce a round bundle of scarlet berries subtended by a whorl of typical parallel-veined leaves.

Wake Robin

But spring really begins with trillium, the crisp white lily that opens so early that it has come by the common name of wake robin. I set out one morning on a trail blazed by our friend Ivill Kelbaugh, in search of a pile of cedar posts he had cut years ago for Bob Higgins, the owner of the place called Higgins Cove. Having nothing more appropriate at hand, Ivill had marked the trail with pages from a magazine impaled on twigs and stubs.

Many of the pages had blown away during the winter of rain, but the trail was still evident with a little searching. I had taken along a pocket full of torn cotton strips for more permanent marking, and I paused often to tie these and to search for trillium. As the woods thickened but showed less undergrowth, the terrain turned downgrade. Ancient and rotting stumps dented by long-ago ax blades wore tophats of unrolling sword fern and tall red huckleberry, or were draped from top to base with the light-green egg-shaped leaves of salal, a plant prized by west coast Indians for its dark purple, mealy berries and by brushpickers and packers for the beauty and long-lasting quality of its evergreen foliage.

The trail ended. The posts, deteriorated through the years, made up a mound of softened wood in which trailing wild blackberries had found a foothold. A little way farther, I was confronted by a length of fence fashioned from hand-hewn cedar pickets. Some of the pickets had fallen and were lost in growth, trailing wild blackberry, mahonia, and salal. But entire sections still stood intact, the pickets held together by lengths of planed lumber and bits of rusted wire, the curved grain weathered to a soft gray patina. I recalled having heard that goats were once kept on the place. How a goat could be confined by a four-foot fence I have no notion. Tempered by years of weathering and seasons of growth, this evidence of man's handiwork had become a part of the woods and did not seem an intrusion.

Beyond the fence a path materialized and led steeply downward, to terminate suddenly in a hollow at the base of a half-live hemlock, a small round low-ceilinged aperture carpeted with layers of leaves and needles. Something, a raccoon perhaps, must sleep out its days here. No tracks showed in the velvety duff. I searched the high branches but could see nothing. Occasionally, a small raccoon face peers out from hiding and reminds me of "find the faces" exercises in children's picture books.

Now, finally, trillium bloomed in profusion on the moist side of the gulch. I counted ten, a dozen crisp white blossoms. Some stood knee high on long slender stems. Others that had barely cleared the brown leaf cushions still wore the leaves like rakish hats. No matter how closely I watch for the first emergence of leaf and stem, I rarely find these plants before bud or flower appears. It is as though they spring up, literally, overnight, and come to flower between sundown and sunrise.

The name, trillium, comes from the arrangement of leaf and flower—three leaves, three green sepals, three white petals, six dark stamens. Even the stigma is tri-lobed. The pure white corolla, with pointed petals, rises on a short stem above a whorl of leaves, a specimen flower, an entire bouquet. As days pass into weeks the petals turn to palest pink, which deepens to rose purple or to a dark maroon. Even after the petals have fallen away, the three green sepals held erect above three green leaves hold a flower shape.

Bulbs lie deep underground and appear to deepen each year, a fact that may explain the sturdiness of the stalk. I am tempted to take home a flower or two, for they keep well indoors. But the blossom must mature on the plant in order to be repeated. During my first spring in Washington a friend brought a trillium, bulb and all, planted in a pottery cup. Each year, in the flower bed outside, the flowers increased in number. When we sold the house after eighteen years, I exhumed the cluster of bulbs and brought them to the Island to plant in the shade of the Lambert cherry. Some springs see twelve to fifteen flowers from the single beginning.

Another common name, birthroot, had its origin from the midwestern custom of using the thick underground rootstocks as an aid in childbirth. The bulb has been used by certain modern-day Northwest Indian tribes as a love potion, according to Erna Gunther in *Ethnobotany of Western Washington*. The root, a thick potatolike tuber, is set with many rootlets. Botanists explain that the plant hurries to its conclusion before the spring-burgeoning forest canopy shuts out sunlight necessary to its propagation. On the slopes where the flowers grew and bloomed that spring day, red alder was coming into leaf, tall, leaning trees that would presently form a nearly solid canopy. And so the wake robin must hurry on its way to maturity.

Farewell, Juncos

One morning I stood for a long moment in puzzled contemplation of the feeding board and the earth beneath. From daybreak until dark, all through the winter, the patch of ivy in which the board stands had been alive with movement. The grain put out the previous day remained untouched. A solitary towhee scratched in the leaves beside the myrtle. A sparrow sang softly from the Philadelphus.

Of course! The juncos that had been with us since October had departed for nesting grounds in the mountains. For them, migration is a matter of altitude. Each year I think I will peg the exact day of their departure, but I never have. Flockers by disposition, they give no notice, as robins and swallows do, of impending departure. One day they are thick on the feeder and among the ivy leaves. The next day they are gone. We will not see them again until October. I wonder whether we get the same individuals year after year. They come so unerringly to the feeding tables.

Some years a solitary junco, or a pair, remains throughout the summer. I wonder why these stay behind and ponder the apparent change in social behavior. In numbers, juncos are quarrelsome birds. Unlike the finches, which feed peacefully together, they fly at other species and attack each other, taking belligerent turns at the feeding board. But in minority, they wait patiently for second table, feed on the fringes, dip quickly in the bath and retire to the holly branches to dry their rumpled shoulder capes.

During a visit to snow line on the slopes of Mount Rainier one summer, I observed a flock of juncos feeding with band-tailed pigeons on the mineral flats and in among red osier dogwood. They looked dear and familiar, old friends with whom I had spent the winter; and for a moment I, too, felt a sense of having migrated to higher levels.

Erythronium

On a bright, still day I turned off the road and walked up the hill to the Island burial ground to look for *Erythronium,* the dog-tooth violet with spotted leaves, a regal little lily that deserves a sweeter name. The CEMETERY sign at the foot of the hill on Eckenstam-Johnson Road had fallen during the winter, blown over, or been spirited away by some curio seeker. Only the white post remained. The loss did not matter much. Islanders, whose dead lie in the hidden graveyard above, know the location well enough, and the sign tended to attract only that singular breed for which *any* burial ground holds interest.

The access road, lined with brush on either side, was rutted from winter rains, which had made rivulets of the ruts, cutting them deeper and deeper until the entire road was awash. Dogwood trees, little more than shrub height on the rocky hillside, were in full white bloom. The front fence, fallen and broken the last time I visited, had been rolled up and taken away, as had the hand-engraved wooden sign. The road turned in and circled out, making a loop, to descend the hill again. The entire front was open. I could see that deer had wandered among the darkened stones on paths of their own making, to browse the leaves from roses and chrysanthemums planted on individual graves, perhaps to seek shelter from the rain in the open "chapel."

The *Erythronium* was in bloom. In the border beyond the stones that huddle together in community, surrounded by wild growth, drifts of the neat white lilies with golden anthers and pointed petals spread farther each spring and grow more numerous. Some call the plant fawn lily or trout lily. Canadians say "Easter lily," and so did we as children. Varieties differ little as to marking of leaf or petal. When we found these lilies blooming in the draws in southeast Kansas, we knew that spring had come.

As spring, and then summer, advanced, *Erythronium* opened gradually at higher and higher altitudes, sometimes yellow but most often white, always with recurved petals. In the Rocky Mountains of Colorado we found them blooming in July at ten thousand feet on the edge of snow-banks. On Mount Rainier they may be found in August along the margins of glaciers, giving rise to the additional names of glacier lily or avalanche lily. Adder's tongue and deer's tongue are common names that describe the leaves.

Unlike most lilies, they grow in patches. I have not found them all here, but I have learned where to look . . . near the site of the old beaver dam on Schoolhouse Creek, behind the mallard hole above East Oro Bay, on a slope in the vicinity of Carlson Cove. On the overgrown meadow at Jacobs' Point, *Erythronium* is still in bloom during the first week in May close by the sharp-edged blades of *Sisyrinchium* (which hold aloft bright blue, three-petaled flowers) we know as blue-eyed grass. This small, gay, wet-meadow flower of the iris family is not plentiful here, or if it is, I have not found it.

Green Power

Despite the fact (readily admitted) that I derive both benefit and pleasure these late years from the all-weather roads that have replaced some of the washed and dusty thoroughfares here on the Island, I experience a certain satisfaction each spring from seeing man's work undone by uncurling fronds of bracken fern and stout-hearted fungi that bulge and then break through rock and asphalt to complete a stubborn growth cycle commenced in the darkness of the earth below.

Walking these roads in April, I see the telltale hump

or blister in the paving. Each successive day the blister increases a little until a crack appears. A loop of green or brown or cream emerges. The crack widens. A leaf or a cap advances and pushes upward. Man's work crumbles away. If his machines were by some circumstance evacuated from the freeways and highways of America, how long before these roads would revert to forest or to prairie?

And so it is with the abandoned farmsteads on the Island. Several have been completely taken over, so that no trace remains. The house stood here, or here, old timers say, beside the lake or beside the creek. Wasps and bees move in, followed by spiders, chipmunks, mice, and rats. Clothing and paper are chewed for nesting material. Wood is perforated. Beetles and ants invade decaying matter. Quietly, without fanfare, nature takes over.

Of flora, once-domestic Himalaya blackberries, European species, make the initial invasion, sending long thorny arms through breaks and crevices. Oregon evergreen blackberry, even thornier, follows. Trailing wild blackberries have an affinity for wood, and take advantage of rich soil around old poultry houses and barns. Wild blackcap, black raspberries with blue stems, literally march through the ruins, arch over, and take root at the tips. Alder and bracken push through any interstice between the floor boards. Within at least one Islander's memory, his birthplace has become forest.

Given leeway, nature goes about her work methodically. Driving around the Island on sightseeing tours, as we did prior to our entrenchment here, strangers are puzzled by the numbers of obviously unused poultry houses, the neglected and abandoned orchards, stark evidence of the change in "small farming," the braking down of Island inhabitants as the years pass. Barns and outsheds have fallen in and are overgrown with Himalaya and honeysuckle.

Orchards were tended once, sprayed and pruned, the fruit sold on the mainland. Farmers had their own hand-

crank and hand-squeeze cider presses, their own huckleberry cleaners. These are relics now. Each year takes its
toll of fruit trees as well as of people. Ricks of apple wood
mark the site. Or trees lie where they have fallen, bleached
gray skeletons with roots upthrust. Firs spring up. Blessed
by sun and light, a teeming forest begins again where
forest stood less than a century ago.

But in March and April, living trees planted by men
long since dead burst forth in a cloud of fragrant pink and
white blossom. Plum trees gone wild spill out of confine-
ment and make thickets of their own. Hybrid forms of
bitter cherry spring up in clusters near old orchards, bloom
white in April, bear fruit for wild birds, and serve as lures
for the moths of tent caterpillars to deposit eggs among the
branches.

Fallen and decaying fruit having conditioned the soil to
their liking, edible morels appear in these uncultivated
areas, some years in abundance. To me, these little pine-
cone-shaped mushrooms are not as tasty as the *Agaricus*
that pops up in open fields when temperatures have
dropped and rains have fallen sufficiently in September or
October. But Islanders wax enthusiastic about their flavor
and secretive about their habitat. As notional as any mushroom, they grow profusely one year and decline to put in an
appearance the next.

In one of these orchards, crocus in a variety of colors
carpets the slope beneath mostly dead trees, blooming
among English daisies and daffodils that creep farther and
farther from gardens no longer remembered. Along the
fringes, balsamroot with big heart-shaped leaves blooms
bright gold in April, miniature sunflowers among ubiqui-
tous dandelions that swarm with sulphur-yellow goldfinches, a symphony in golds and yellows. Showy and restless, the finches undulate from flower to flower, dipping
and rising, the tiny males bright yellow and black in spring
regalia, the females olive-cream with black wings and white

wing bars. A butterfly the color of forsythia comes to complete the composition.

I would like to say a word here and now for the English daisy. Few American wildflower guides give it so much as a nod. Despised by the lawn-proud, it suffers a drenching with 2-4-D, or is dredged out along with hairy cat's ear and plantain and sorrel. Even the *Oxford Book of Wildflowers* dismisses the diminutive daisy as "a very common weed of lawns . . . in the British Isles, flowering practically the whole year."

And so it does. I do not recall a single time here, save when snows covered the ground, that I could not walk a few steps from the door and find this cheerful white or pink or lavender-rose "day's eye" blooming underfoot. Ask any child whether English daisy is a weed. For making daisy chains it has no equal.

Moss Gathering

As though to remind us that spring was not altogether a chronological fact of the calendar, big soft flakes of snow fell. Gray-green water was dotted by whitecaps that ran before a north wind and windrows of kelp and sea lettuce in meandering lines along the beach were frosted with foam. Bird song ceased and birds disappeared in cover of pine and fir and holly. The few gulls that coasted on cold air kept close to protected shallows.

Deer had come in the night and had cut all the tulips to ground level but had touched neither daffodils nor crocus. All through the night long beaded catkins from the cottonwood tree had bombarded the roof, and by morning catkins covered roof and earth. The sun came out and the snow vanished. I went into the woods to gather moss for the fuchsia baskets.

Around the spring where the moss grew thick, pale

brown fertile stems of horsetail bore dark brown fruiting cones, each joint decorated by a fringe of scales in a loose sheath, like a tiny miniskirt. Later, when they had shed their spores, the fertile stems would give way to sterile stalks with green fronds and wirelike branches.

Among the oldest living plants, distantly related to ferns, horsetails grow almost worldwide. Fossilized "leaves" of horsetail have been found in coal beds deep underground. Throughout the summer and into autumn these queer, nonflowering forerunners border cool shaded roadsides and soften the contours of tidal ditches where soil is wet and brackish. In a bare soggy patch below the spring, ridged silicate shoots of scouring rush stood like swords thrust into moist earth. Swarms of mosquitoes arose from among a jungle of skunk cabbage.

In an opening where a big hemlock had gone down years before and was turning to earth again, a cluster of brown cup fungi without stems or gills resembled tiny oval leather bowls, smooth inside and out as though shaped on a fairy wheel. I find that these cuplike receptacles sometimes contain spore capsules attached by threads, like bead-size eggs deposited in nests.

The spring is surrounded by concrete housing, grown over now with spongy cushions of moss that peels off in sheets. The moss makes a quick comeback following harvest, as do the various mosses that coat decaying logs and clothe the stream banks. Some feel dry and abrasive, others cool and silky. Used as lining for wire baskets, they turn brown in sunshine but green again when rains come and days darken.

Having filled my carryall with cool green rolls, I came out into the sunshine again. A flock of evening grosbeaks swept past and settled in a broadleaf maple with pale yellow bloom, as though the tree had suddenly borne ripe fruit. These visits are rare, for we are out of the normal flight pattern. I wondered what had brought them to detour across the water. A few pecked at leftover samara, the dry double-winged seed pods of the maple. But most simply moved about with restless hops and flutters and much communication. The air was filled with clear whistled calls.

Chunky birds, with pale, thick, seed-cracking beaks (hence the name of "gross beak"), they undulate in flight as do the finches. Sometimes we see them once or twice in the spring, and again in the fall, some years not at all. Once a flock descended into the hawthorn tree and remained for half a day feeding on the fruits and bathing in the birdbath.

The air was damp and raw as I approached the water, and smelled of snow. Finding only one salamander on the road, headed for the swamp, I guessed that the spring migration of these little fellows had neared an end and that he was laggard. I took him up and carried him to safety, but he lashed his tail and twisted in an effort to escape. If man ever contrives to establish a universal language, I wish it might be broadened to include all species. The salamander would know, then, that I wished him well. Perhaps, in turn, *he* might be able to tell *me* what motivates his journey.

Somewhere far back from the road, a pileated woodpecker kept up a steady knocking. I finally located him. His red cockade shone in the sunlight. His tail was clamped tightly against the ragged bark of a half-dead cedar that stood ten to twenty feet above its companions. Food source and shelter to a variety of life besides the pileated, the tree would stand another decade or so I reckoned, barring man's blind intervention.

A buck and doe watched my passage from a greening meadow and went back to browse. April usually begins fawning time, but perhaps this doe was barren. A rufous-sided towhee piped a clear note from a moss-topped fence post and flew away. Down the road ahead, a long-tailed killdeer ran and stopped and ran again, obviously more from habit than with purpose. Many species, including sandpipers, and, to some extent, robins, use this technique, if technique it is, for baffling and mystifying a possible

enemy. In water, flounders employ the same ruse for confusing the beholder. We are all full of ruses. How little we know, really, about each other's motivations. How helplessly inarticulate we are, even among our own species.

Cuckoldry in the Bird World

As spring deepened brown-headed cowbirds appeared in increasing numbers. The iridescent green-black males with dull brown heads and characteristic swagger outnumbered the mouse-gray females two or three to one. A certain pairing off was apparent. Males made courting gestures to selected females, bowed, strutted, ruffled feathers. But a great many bachelors also visited the feeder and paid no attention to the ladies. A female brown-head has a furtive look. These few pecked nervously along the edges of the board, responding to the preening males coolly or not at all, and spooked at the slightest disturbance.

Nesting instincts of the little *Molothrus ater* would seem one of nature's bungles. Like Old World cuckoos, cowbirds are parasitic. Having located a nest to her liking, usually (though not always) that of a smaller species, the fertilized female deposits her egg therein and flies away to rejoin her husband. At some time during five or six ensuing days she repeats the performance, generally in other nests, wherever she can find a repository unguarded. Given space and opportunity, she may add a second egg to the original. Obligation fulfilled, the irresponsible pair rejoins the flock.

Certain ornithologists advance an interesting theory to explain this unseemly and irregular behavior on the part of cowbirds (if not of cuckoos). Being disinclined to believe that nature (however devious) is capable of real evil, I am inclined to give the theory a certain credence. In the days before barbed wire, so say the theorists, cowbirds in numbers followed buffalo herds across the plains, feeding on ticks on the animals' backs and on flies and other insects rousted from the grass by the herd's progress, as these birds follow domestic animals today. Mutually beneficial as the exchange and collaboration proved to be, the steady advance across the prairie of nomad bison afforded the small benefactors insufficient time for such domestic pursuits as home building and tending of posterity. Other, smaller birds provided a solution. Once established, the cheeky practice continued.

Young cowbirds, hatched and reared by unsuspecting foster parents, formed their own flocks. Females parasitized in their turn, and the colony moved on. So close was this association between birds and animals that the wanderers became known as "buffalo birds." As buffaloes diminished on the plains and domestic cattle increased in numbers, necessitating for *Molothrus* a switch in providers, the name was changed to "cowbird." Less sympathetic observers called them "cuckolds."

Cowbirds have been known to parasitize up to 150 species. These include various sparrows, warblers, and vireos; but the big speckled eggs of this interloper have also been found in nests of catbirds, thrashers, and robins, even of hawks and seagulls, from which they are quickly ejected. A chalk-up for robin intelligence lies in the fact that the female robin, finding a brown-speckled egg in her blue clutch, tosses the misfit overside.

Nor do all the smaller cuckolded accept such gifts without protest. Warblers (a favorite victim, perhaps because they are so numerous) have been known to floor over a cowbird's egg, even though they may eliminate their own in the process. Indeed, warblers' nests have been found to contain several such floors, with a cowbird's egg walled away beneath each construction. Should a cowbird commit the error of depositing a first egg in a newly-finished nest, the owner may abandon the structure and start another.

However these little dramas of the bird world began, they generally have a tragic ending for the duped. Having departed the egg a few days early (a short gestation period being part and parcel, too, of nature's enigmatical plan), the illegitimate offspring calls loudly for attention. Adult birds neglect their own in a vain attempt to still the insistent cries of the impostor. Even after he has outgrown the nest, the little monster continues to demand and to receive attention. His nestmates (provided he has not already evicted them over the side) may well be left to die of malnutrition. I have seen chipping sparrows practically stand on tiptoe in order to thrust food into the gaping bills of cowbird young. I reckoned that fledglings might be dying in a nest somewhere but had no knowledge of the location. Having attained full size, this ungrateful creature flies away to join his own kind, to begin his own irresponsible life in their association.

The toll taken of desirable species by such unseemly behavior would be difficult to determine. Even the loss of song must be considerable. The cowbird's wheezing whistle can hardly be termed a melody. On the other hand, this pariah of the bird world is not without his defenders. Seed and insect eaters, cowbirds are said to account for the demise of vast numbers of pests, including crickets and tent caterpillars. I cannot vouch for this, never having seen *any* bird approach the repulsive masses of tent caterpillars that infest the trees. But we do see them in numbers feeding on weed seeds in lawn and pasture. And certainly their penchant for flies and ticks must be a boon to the grazing animals with which they associate. Having once drowned, in anger, a female cowbird caught in the act of depositing a big intrusive egg in a small warbler's nest (or so we are told), John Burroughs, the famous naturalist, suffered pangs of remorse over having upset nature's balance. Cowbirds (he called them "cow buntings"), he reasoned, were, after all, a part of the plan, not well understood perhaps, but to be tolerated.

May

The Shore Road

As I walked along a shore road I was assailed all at once
by the delightful fragrance of wild plum. So far as I know,
no plum grows in the vicinity. But I have observed often
along this road that mingled aromas are like a medley, a
chorus, blended together in scarcely identifiable harmony
—plum, oso, ginger, salt, iodine, laurel.

In some ways the road is an unfortunate circumstance,
a divider between house and beach that we would like to
wish away. But it must be remembered that when agriculture was a means of livelihood here, boats were a necessary
factor and beaches were access. Privacy was a plentiful
commodity then. View was secondary, or taken for granted.

Truthfully, I do not mind the road. The shore curves
and the road follows, a dividing line between sea and land.
Gulls and sandpipers rarely cross over. Killdeer nest on this
side. The green bank between is a median strip; when the
wind is high and from north by east, flora that has struck

root there is misted by salt spray. Pussywillow and (appropriately) ocean spray, little wild cherry, evergreen blackberry, alder seedling, wild rose, and numerous other varieties have found a foothold. The bank ranges from "nobank" to twenty feet or more in height, broadens and narrows and broadens again. Coarse grasses, reeds and sedges, horsetail and samphire, and sturdy stalks of gumweed, all salt-tolerant, fringe the shore of the nameless tide creek. At times of high wind and high tide, the sea invades the flat, creeps or dashes across the road, so that, ferry bound, we are obliged to take the long way around. Receding, waters leave a whitened residue, a flat rich with mineral and salt, where interesting and strange flora thrive.

On the hill, high above the water, where the median widens and brush thickens, mountain balm (or sticky laurel) comes into fragrant bloom in late April. Heads of small white flowers that make a soapy lather when dipped in water open among glossy, evergreen, parallel-veined leaves. Botanists say the soapy characteristic comes from saponin, a poisonous glucoside. Prior to my coming to the Island I had not seen or at least been aware of the shrub. When I asked its identity, I was told it was "greasewood," a good-enough name. The odd curled-in leaves are covered with a gummy substance with a pungent, aromatic odor. Whether fragrant or simply "smelly," I have never been able to decide. Rub a leaf between your fingers and the stickiness and the odor remain for a long time. Indians used the leaves as a substitute for tobacco.

In the woods the shrub grows to eight or ten feet and blooms later in the season. Limbs turn upward, reaching for sunlight. Under warm sun, the leaves curl inward to conserve moisture, to lessen exposed surface. The underside of the leaves is velvet soft. *Ceanothus velutinus,* it goes by many names—mountain laurel, snowbrush, deerbrush, tobacco brush, and soapbloom. Flowers in masses *do* resemble snowflakes. Where the shrub grows thick, as in the Rocky Mountains, it is said that overbrowsing by deer is a sign of overpopulation but I do not recall ever having seen any indication that the plant serves as deer browse here.

Albert, the Good

April, this past year, was a month of real, not false spring. As I walked down the road to fetch the evening paper, a pleasant chore, the air smelled of earth freshly-turned and of the newly mowed grass in Mr. Backstrom's garden.

On the previous day I had attended Sunday school in the Island chapel, built in the edge of a fir wood. The words of one of the hymns, a traditional English melody by Maltbie Babcock, remained with me. They seemed especially appropriate for April: "All nature sings, and 'round me rings / The music of the spheres."

The first of the orchard trees to bloom had commenced to drop their petals. The slightest breeze brought a shower of petals that appeared to dance to the accompaniment of a glass wind chime suspended from a branch of the Wealthy apple tree. On a high twig, a purple finch in spring dress added to the shower by plucking petals so as to get at the immature fruit, playing his own game of "she-loves-me." On days with no wind stirring this little finch betrays his presence among the blossoms by this methodical counting drop.

As I entered the house the phone rang. "This is St. Joseph's Hospital," a strange voice said when I had identified myself. "Your friend Albert has just died." I thanked her and hung up. The news was not totally unexpected. Knowing that his condition was critical following an operation, I had gone to see Albert earlier in the day. I had been pleased to see that he seemed not to be suffering and that he appeared to be holding his own. We had exchanged a few words. When I asked whether he needed anything he shook his head. Lately, his skin had worn a transparent pallor that contrasted strongly with his customary rugged outdoor coloring. That afternoon his color had been high, his eyes bright blue and clear, his crooked grin somehow reassuring.

"He never complains," a nurse told me, outside. "He's always asking whether *we* get enough rest. When he has to turn on his light he apologizes for giving trouble. We've never had a patient like him here." She promised to let me know. I think they were all surprised by the number of friends who called, people for whom he had done yard work over the years, employees from the tavern-cafe downtown where he took most of his meals. These latter kept an eye on him as he grew older and began to ail. One of the girls had called me when he fell ill in the cheerless room where he made his home. She had found my name in a magazine he had taken to read.

I went outside and walked about the yard and looked at the work Albert had done. He loved the Island and had come at intervals for twenty years, making the two-hour trip by bus and ferry from downtown Tacoma. Sometimes he showed up unexpectedly, especially in winter, when odd jobs slacked off. Too proud to ask for work, or to accept charity, he simply appeared at the door, a grin on his face, a flower or a sprig of holly in the stained band of his hat. He knew well enough we always had work that needed doing, and, as a sop to his pride, I went along with the pretense.

As he worked, he talked to himself, or he groaned like a man in travail. Whether spading, pruning, or weeding, any job he finished was without flaw. He loved to work with rocks, setting and resetting heavy stones until he was satisfied with the effect. Wherever I looked, now, I saw evidence of this achievement in his studied arrangement of close-ranked stones.

Whether or not he understood the meaning of the word, he was an environmentalist. His love for growing things could only be described as dedication. As did another Albert (of Lambarine), he respected all life. When I complained that the deer damaged the young fruit trees or the mock orange, he said mildly, "All they do is prune a little. Things *need* pruning." He disapproved of my war against garden slugs. "Slugs got to live, too," he reminded me.

He could never bring himself to throw away a bulb or root with blooming potential. If one employer ran out of space, he carried the surplus to the next. He rarely came to the Island without a pack on his back, a sack of bulbs, a discarded forsythia, a no-longer-wanted rose, a tangle of iris rhizomes, a bundle of chrysanthemum shoots. *We* had plenty of room. He spaded a new bed, "borrowed" manure from an absent neighbor's barn, painstakingly planted his unsolicited gift.

Occasionally I grumbled to myself. But looking about, now, I saw King Alfred daffodils of incredible size, lovely Mount Hood, dainty Thalia, poet's narcissus, monument and memorial to his devotion—to them, not to us—specimens he would never see in flower.

"Albert, the Good," one widowed employer called him. He called himself "Monty." Where he had come from no one knew. He made up little lives for himself, in Montana, Alaska, Colorado, England, even Australia. He boasted no surviving relatives. So far as we knew he had never owned so much as a garden nor had access to a piece of land he could call his own. But he was both skilled and knowledgeable in the lore of living plants. When outdoor work slackened, he scrubbed floors, washed windows, cleaned walls, even babysat. Children and animals trusted him. As he weeded next door, he moved a happy baby girl from flower bed to flower bed in her pushcart.

He had his own notion of sharing. If I were out of peat or fertilizer, he helped himself from the neighbors' sheds, or he came from the neighbors to take what he needed from our supply. "Don't do any good in the sack," he mumbled. His first concern was the good earth and the roots it nourished. Three weeks prior to his death, at eighty-two, he climbed high into the crown to prune the apple tree. I trembled, but knew better than to protest.

When I was hospitalized briefly the following December, one of his floor nurses saw my name on the admissions list and came upstairs to see me. "You're Monty's friend?" she asked. I was happy to acknowledge the fact. "We've never forgotten him," she said. Indigent, unprepossessing, considerate Albert, the Good, had been one of a vast turnover whom she remembered.

Evening Song

As rains slackened and daylight hours lengthened, sunrise and sunset over the water seemed personal dispensations. Of mornings the sun appeared, an orange-red balloon, a little to the left of snow-draped Mount Rainier. The fiery ball peered, crescent-shaped, above the blue foothills of the Cascades, and then bounced, entire, into a Confederate-gray sky. A brilliant bridge materialized across the channel, from mainland to Island. The day began and ran its course. The sun dropped behind the Olympic Range. Evening red faded slowly from the sky. Mount Rainier changed from coral pink to a ghostly gray and melted from view.

After the evening chores were done I climbed the long hill and walked the mile or so along Guthrie Road to listen to the frog chorus that came up from the waters of the swamp below. I could hear no individual voice, and yet it was as though each tried to outdo the other. The resultant collective harmony was both beautiful and deafening. I could have listened all night.

As I came this way, through the woods, the sound grew less but lost no harmony. The road narrowed and leveled, became a cut between tall trees. A pale moon showed the way. Frog song was lost. The silence was so intense I could hear my own footsteps, my own breathing. Earlier, I had come up on several nights to listen to the great horned owl. Now, having nested probably, he was silent. A doe appeared in the road, a gray wraith, and stood with her head raised, as though she had caught my scent or heard my footsteps. I stopped and she moved on.

A breeze whispered through the firs, and the fires that had smoldered and smoked all day sprang into life and cast a flickering glow over newly slashed road clearings. The low mournful tremolo of a screech owl came from far off. The humped shadowy figures of two adult raccoons materialized out of the woods, headed for the swamp, in search of food for their young I reckoned. The young, newly born and still blind probably, would remain in the den in some hollow tree until midsummer. This time of year, before the fruit had ripened, I supposed frogs must provide a good percentage of the coon diet. But I know they dine of nights, too, on the big fresh-water mussels that lie on the sand and mud in the shallow waters of the lakes.

Now the voices of frogs in lesser numbers came from the lakeshore, with an occasional voice, as though tuning up, from the road ditch, a trial run, a sleepy sound. A wan moon broke through the clouds and the road turned silver. All I could see of the sky overhead was a lane dotted with stars. I felt the road turn downward toward Yoman Point. From somewhere on dark water came the faint sound of a work boat, and then the long drawn whistle of a locomotive and the rumble of freight cars on Steilacoom trestle.

A killdeer swept over, crying his name aloud. Reflected lights from Tacoma and from Steilacoom and McNeil Island shone through still-bare trees. A bat, the first I had seen, darted across at eye level, followed by another. It is said that bats emit sounds as they fly and are guided by the echo, sounds too high-pitched for human ears but bouncing back like radar beams from flying insects that serve as food, from monstrous me, an object to be avoided. Was this a pair perhaps, their fancy turned to thoughts of love? Creatures of the night, they seemed mere shadow, without reality or substance.

Last of the "R" Months

In April, the last of the "r" months until September, oysters from the beach seemed even tastier than during the winter, and we were blessed with low daylight tides for harvest. I do not know how the saying came about that oysters are edible only during months with "r" in the spelling. They may be a trifle milkier, a bit thinner (if an oyster can be thin, or fat). But it seems to me that oysters from cold Sound waters vary little from January through December. *We* eat them the year around.

Some must place credence in the theory; during the summer I find fewer poachers on the beach. Perhaps the word "poacher" is not well chosen. One might argue, with considerable fairness, that a native oyster—like a clam, a mussel, a geoduck—is a gift from the sea. Certain Island beaches, such as this one at Yoman Point, support no oysters. Less salt-tolerant than many seashore animals, oysters thrive in more protected waters, diluted by fresh water for at least a portion of the year. Only in recent years have they appeared "wild" on any Island beach.

I use the word "poacher" narrowly, to cover those who load gunny sacks, cartons, bushel baskets, tubs, with no consideration for the difficult fact of reproduction; those who roast the animals in the shell, destroying untold numbers of young in the process. Oysters reproduce by means of eggs that hatch into ciliated free-swimming larvae known as "fry." As with most marine life, a mere fraction of the millions of eggs produced will hatch, only a small percentage of larvae survive to reach maturity. In these cold Sound waters, oysters by no means reproduce every year. Beds invaded by poachers have been all but depleted, others dangerously diminished. Many unattached are lost and broken. Predators take their toll. Some years I see very little spat; other years, none at all.

Among the most interesting bivalves on Island shores is the rock oyster or jingle, *Pododesmus macroschisma,* that leaves delicate, irregular, round shells, the lower valve marked by a circular hole through which has passed the byssus that attached the animal to a supporting rock or shell. The shells of the jingle are unequal, the top valve deep, to cradle its owner. I find the lower valves on pilings, even among seaweed, still firmly attached. When the animal dies, the upper valve is set free, but the lower may remain firmly cemented in deep water.

These are community lives, stacked in layers, interlocked and interdependent. "In all the world of living things," Rachel Carson wrote, "it is doubtful whether there is a more delicately balanced relationship than that of island life to its environment." To be sure, this is true of seashore life, as of forest life, everywhere. On a small sparsely settled island the fact of interdependence seems more apparent, perhaps because it also embraces man. And yet, as Miss Carson has pointed out, it is on islands that man has written one of his blackest records, destroying entire environments by cutting, clearing, and burning.

The Upward Climb

So much had emerged into leaf and bloom during the first warm days that the return trip up the long ascending

trail from the cove took a long time. Even during the winter months the gentle climb is rewarding because there is
so much to see. I think often of Bob and Nella Higgins,
who made the ascent so often during twenty years of own-
ership. Bob is gone now, and Nella does not come any
more. She prefers to remember the paths they took together. Knowing this, I feel a sense of trust, as I hope those
who come after me will feel, that the path should be left
unchanged, that it is only ours for a time, that it belongs
not to us but to all of the natural life that grows and dwells
there—to the deer and the raccoons that daily negotiate the
trail, to the hummingbird that comes to feed on the flowering currant, to the kingfisher and the pigeon guillemot
that nest in the bank, to the great satin-limbed madroña
that towers above the path. I think, sometimes, there will
be a last time for me, as there has been for others. I hope
I may be able to let it go with grace.

In shaded moist places along the trail a smaller species of
Oregon grape, a *Berberis* with lighter, creamier clusters of
bloom, had come into flower. Here where the earth is
spongy with leaf and needle drop and the decay of old
wood, the plant is shallow-rooted. Once I might have suc-
cumbed to the temptation to pull up a specimen or two to
take home, for the sake of the rich russet color the holly-
like leaves will turn in October. But this mahonia does not
take well to a change of environment, and enough has been
destroyed already.

The big maple-shaped leaves of sweet coltsfoot had not
appeared as yet, but the round pale pink heads stood tall on
their scaled stalks and perfumed the air above masses of
unfolding vanilla leaf like the wings of butterflies or of
newly emerged moths, the color a tender green of new
growth. The red-flower currant, as though it had deliberately chosen the site, displayed its blossoms against a background of fir boughs. Oso-berry had been in bloom for a

month but gave no sign of going over. Where the path turned and widened, long yellow pendants of broadleaf maple bloom gave an illusion of sunlight.

Down below, masses of red-berry elder were covered with pyramidal heads of creamy bloom. *Sambucus callicarpa,* this first of the elders comes far in advance of *Sambucus glauca,* the blue-berry elder, still standing bare and winterish in drier woods. By the time the latter comes to bloom, *callicarpa* will be bright with the smooth red berries beloved by band-tailed pigeons.

Some authorities warn that red-berry elder is reputed to be poisonous. But Northwest Indians of many or perhaps all tribes have long used both plants and berries for food and medicine, and pigeons are not given to reading. Deer, too, are said to eat the berries, though they grow out of reach of all save the tallest. A different variety of red-berry elder, *Sambucus pubens,* with orange-red or scarlet fruits, grows at high altitudes in the Rocky Mountains. I have seen it in berry there.

Elders in some variety would appear to grow in almost every section of the country. Some forty species have been catalogued from north to south and east to west, all with pithy stems and all bearing fruit. The Kansas species I knew as a child, *Sambucus canadensis,* grew in Verdigris River bottomland. Each autumn we made a day's excursion by horse and buggy from our upland farm to gather the purple-black fruit for pies that had a smoky taste and were filled with seeds. At the same time we gathered sweet wild grapes, persimmons, papaws. Best of all, we brought home elder stems, reamed out the pithy center, and fashioned popguns and whistles, or experimented with crude flutelike instruments that produced a recorder kind of sound, beautiful to our uncultured ears.

Flower and Fruit

Nights turned mild to match the days. Honeysuckle was in full leaf—the occasional blue fly (*Lonicera coerulea*) with reddish bark and hairy leaves, the eared and slightly hirsute *L. hispidula,* abundant *L. ciliosa*—climbing and twisting, the stems thrust cunningly through disks of upper leaves. The "bloom" on the leaves rubs off and has a floury feel. The name *Lonicera* honors Adam Lonicer, a German botanist.

Flowers of *ciliosa* vary from orange to butterscotch to yellow, crossed, I suspect, with the masses of domestic honeysuckle that have long survived the planter. I find these latter around almost every abandoned house and barn, growths that become heavier each year and soften and sweeten the ruins to which they cling.

A lover of shady places, *ciliosa* emerges as a shrub with thin stems arising from the earth. But then each stem becomes a vining tendril. Stems twine about each other to form a stout cable that may run twenty feet or more, climbing over neighboring species to reach light and air. By September or October the long tubular fringed flowers will have given place to shining clusters of orange berries subtended above twin leaves like little saucers to hold the fruit.

A rarer species I find sometimes is *Lonicera involucrata,* with yellow flowers and purplish-black berries above red bracts, a charming shrub known as twinberry or as bearberry honeysuckle. As with all honeysuckles, the leaves stand opposite on the stem and the yellow flowers are tubular.

Throughout the blooming season, flowers of honeysuckle along wood margins swarm of evenings with long-tongued moths. It is said that bees sometimes steal nectar by literally

"biting" through the tube. So tightly do the stems of twin-
ing honeysuckle wind about their host that in the British
Isles the plant goes by the name of woodbine.

Visitors from the British Isles frequently remark the similarity of flora to that of their homeland, especially those
from moist, generally mild, temperate areas of England and
Scotland. Searching through wildflower guides for some
unfamiliar species (as in the case of *Corydalis aurea,* mentioned earlier), I frequently find the stranger in *The Oxford Book of Wild Flowers.* Common names are invariably
descriptive and picturesque.

A few years ago a small vining plant with lobed, somewhat maple-shaped leaves, appeared among the rocks that
border the front yard. The first flowers opened in April.
Five-petaled, lavender in color, with cleft lower lip and
spur, they were not unlike tiny snapdragons. The plant
launched out in all directions, clung to and then obscured
the rocks. Flowering continued throughout the summer,
and on to Christmas and New Year's. Seed pods formed
and broke open to reveal nests of seeds, like coarse-ground
pepper.

I began to find new plants here and there. From a single
thin-stemmed sprout, one specimen climbed the steps to the
deck, ran along the base of the rough cedar wall a distance
of ten or twelve feet. Protected there, it bloomed the winter
through. When night temperatures dropped to near freezing, blossoms appeared in even greater numbers among the
bright green, hair-stemmed leaves. In cold weather the un-
dersides of the leaves turned to a rich purple. Raising a com-
pact mass of leaf and bloom, I found a solid drift of black
seeds that ran between wall and deck.

This search ended, too, in the Oxford book, among the
snapdragons (*Antirrhinum*), flowers distinguished by encap-
sulated fruits. The persistent little runner is ivy-leaved toad-
flax (*Cymbalaria muralis*), "common on walls throughout
Britain. . . . As seeds ripen, the flower stalk bends toward

cracks in the wall, into which the seeds fall when the capsule bursts open." I went outside to look. Sure enough, the seed stems at the outer edges of the plant were elongated and curled back, to shed their burden in the only crack available, at the base of the broad vertical cedar boards that make up the siding of the bedroom wall.

By the end of the month, blossoms on Indian plum had withered and turned brown and green berries had formed and hung suspended from wirelike stems on the long arched hoops of spring boughs and twigs. In seepy areas shaded by taller growth, Siberian miner's lettuce and our other, rarer, miner's lettuce, *Claytonia perfoliata* (from the peculiar connate stem leaf that forms a cup or plate below the flower cluster), had come into bloom. The flowers of the former are white with notched petals and red penciled lines, like the grass flowers in Kansas that we called "spring beauties." Oddly enough, the name "spring beauty" is given to *Claytonia perfoliata* in English guidebooks. Another edible *Claytonia* in England is known as "garden purslane."

The leaves of both varieties of miner's lettuce here are succulent, hence the name. The plants are said to have saved goldminers of forty-nine from the scourge of scurvy. Indians gathered leaves and stems of *Claytonia* to heap on ant hills, to give the ants a "sour taste." Erna Gunther reveals that pregnant Quinault women of the Northwest Coast chew entire plants of miner's lettuce "so the baby will be soft when born."

House Hunting

Having long talked of an excursion into a thirty-five-acre wood in search of a house uninhabited for some twenty years, we set out on a Sunday afternoon to try to find it. The fact that we did not find the house that day would hardly seem credible to one unfamiliar with the rapidity with which dense growth can block off a trail and blanket a clearing in this climate.

Knowing well enough that the house was there, we hacked our way through blackberry and nettle, alder seedlings, thorny loops and hoops of wild black raspberry, gooseberry, thimbleberry, huckleberry, salal. Stumps from some early logging venture, covered by earth and green growth, stood like burial mounds for elephants. A great

round burl on a fallen broadleaf maple wore a moss wig inches thick and in a perfect wig shape. In deeper woods, with less undergrowth, decaying logs supported clusters of bird's-nest fungi, cuplike receptacles lined with spore-filled peridioles attached by threads.

We may have traveled in a circle. We lost all sense of direction and were surprised to come suddenly into the open. The beach lay below us, at the foot of a bank of clay so slippery we were hard-pressed to keep footing. Having given up the search for the time, we explored the beach, inaccessible except by boat or by the rugged pathless way we had come.

Water-cut caves along the bank were divided into dripping rooms by the roots of overhanging trees. A great blue heron had left tracks of incredible size in clay-colored mud, footprints that measured six and one-half inches from the tip of the central of three front toes to the end of a hind toe.

We made our way along the beach to an open meadow, the site of another abandoned homestead. I had seen the place from a distance—a sprawl of jumbled buildings, a few broken orchard trees, a shade tree or two, some geometric fencing. From a distance, on a wet winter day, the sight was depressing. The close-up view in late April was charming.

Daffodils by the hundreds spilled golden blossoms in ragged lines along fallen fence rows. Poet's narcissus bloomed among scattered boards and broken window glass, and softened rusted heaps of farm machinery. We peered through paneless windows into half a dozen buildings. Oddly, the final inhabitants seemed to have departed in haste, without bothering to pack belongings. Postcards and letters littered the floor among brochures and magazines, schoolbooks and bulletins. In the kitchen, cups and plates lay among scattered cutlery on an oilcloth-covered table.

Pots and pans occupied a dilapidated stove upon which a brick chimney had fallen.

Alder trees an inch in diameter had come through the floor and had died there. Blackberry and honeysuckle had penetrated the moss-grown roof and window openings. A sagging bedstead complete with mattress and pillows in yellowed cases furnished a downstairs bedroom. The parlor contained a ruined phonograph, a stiff-backed settee with bristling springs and cracked simulated-leather upholstery. A trunk, opened no doubt by earlier trespassers, spilled rotted clothing from which mice had cut nesting material.

This was not my first experience of such abandonment here. I am always at a loss to understand. It is as though the family simply arose from the table and departed, not even bothering to close the door. At one place a skillet stood (and still stands so far as I know) unwashed for twenty years on a rusted collapsed stove. Dried residue of coffee stained a cup. A green silver-plated spoon lay in the saucer. When windows go and the roof caves in, even the mouse smell disappears. Letters, sometimes personal and passionate, litter the floor or overflow from mildewed bureau drawers. Some of these have been spilled, I suppose, by prowlers in search of stamps. But why were they left?

I found a book of love poems in a heap of books on the bed and sat down to read. Who had cared for these, been moved by the tender words? How long ago? I laid the book back and went outside again. China eggs remained in the nests of the poultry house. Harness and sweat-stained pads hung on a barn wall. Broken steps led downward into a roofless caved-in cellar. Darkened canned fruit reposed in still-sealed Mason jars in an open cupboard, along with patent medicines and household remedies.

These places are mostly posted now, and so I rarely trespass. With a recent influx of strangers to the Island, No Hunting and No Trespassing signs have appeared. Some of the better houses have been boarded up. One owner

wisely set fire to the tumbled buildings, discovered by junk
and bottle collectors. Sometimes I wonder how my own
cherished but worthless possesions will be left. The house
has been here for a long time. It cannot last forever. I hope
someone will have the kindness and good sense to burn it
to ground level and rake the ashes flat, so that the spot will
green over and leave no trace.

Arbutus Blight

The water remained blue and calm, reflecting a blue sky.
White clouds formed and reformed patterns on the still

surface. Flow tide crept across the beach and made a colored underwater mosaic, pebbles in tones of emerald and jade green, white, blue, jasper red, yellow, jet black, lovely shades of gray. Flowerlike sun anemones with orange and white tentacles opened among blood-red starfish and clusters of blue mussels on pilings and bridge supports. Transparent jellyfish moved spasmodically through the crystal clear water. At each low tide little water jellyfish (*Aequorea aequorea*) were left stranded on the beach; their radial canals extending from stomach to margin gave them the appearance of glass butter chips. Luminescent after dark, they lent to the night beach a jewel-studded look.

Even at depths of ten feet or more, as we drifted about in skiff or canoe, brilliant red sea cucumbers and strange orange sea pens, like rows of topless carrots thrust point down in the sand, were clearly visible. Hermit crabs moved about in borrowed shells among blood-red sunflower stars and edible crab cousins. Gulls soared and searched. Occasionally a gull dropped into the water, dipped his head, and emerged with a struggling herring.

I do not know just when it was that we began to notice that something had gone wrong with the madroña trees all over the Island. Young trees did not seem so much affected. But dead leaves began to appear among the lower branches of all of the old-timers. Generally the trees are at their best in April, the crowns bright glossy green, with pale chartreuse patches appearing among red-skinned upper limbs. Dead leaves appear at intervals, but are scarcely noticed among new growth. We became aware that no new growth had manifested itself.

As days passed, the blight increased and crept upward, to envelop entire trees. Hardly a sprig of green showed. Even the lovely bark took on a tarnished look. We stood underneath the trees and listened with dismay to a steady rain of stiff dead leaves. Entire rows of old trees looked to be devoid of life. Without the brightness of madroña to break the somberness of conifer, the Island would present a gloomy aspect. Even younger trees began to show damage.

I thought uneasily of a tale told me years ago by a botany student at the university. The madroña tree, his professor had said, is a diseased and dying species that will some day be extinct. The story had alarmed me, and I had tried to trace its origin. A fungus leaf spot might cause defoliation, authorities revealed. But I found nothing to substantiate a theory of probable extinction. "Of one thing you may be certain," a young man who loves madroñas as I do remarked with a trace of bitterness, "if madroña wood was of any *commercial* value, an investigation would be under way, and pronto."

We had underestimated the general public. Deluged by calls and letters from up and down the coast, horticulturists at Washington State University had conducted their own research. The trees were neither dead nor dying, they reported. Nature's balance had simply been upset by the uncommonly hard winter, the unaccustomed lengthy cold the region had suffered. The trees were "temporarily confused." Defoliation had set in unseasonably, and new growth was simply tardy. This stately lover of fog would survive the debacle.

They were quite right. Throughout May and June defoliation continued, and the dying look maintained. Only younger and more protected seedlings put forth feeble clusters of lily-of-the-valley blossom, not all of which matured. But then small tufts of green began to appear among the blackened clinging leaves of even older trees. Day by day sparse green crept upward to clothe the naked crowns, and we breathed more easily. A few late blooms emerged. Small clusters of rough irregular berries formed, began to ripen, and were set upon by cedar waxwings, robins, pileated woodpeckers, and band-tailed pigeons.

Now, more than a year later, the trees have not yet fully

recovered. But they are still on the way. Much seemingly dead wood remains, especially in the lower branches of some of the older specimens. Perhaps certain trees will never recover. As a result, our admiration and pride in this small-range and beautiful tree is intensified. Had the cold lasted a bit longer, what then?

Perhaps it is only my imagination, but it seems to me that madroña seedlings are more numerous this year than I have ever seen them and that they are more vigorous and faster growing, as though to make up for the almost loss. I have been struck by this kind of renewal in nature many times following a hard winter or, more especially, a dry summer, both here and in the Southwest. Locust, cotton-wood, willow, hawthorn, laurel spring up in rock crevices and in dry clay, without benefit of moisture. After a dying black locust (not native to this area) had been cut down here in the yard, locust trees came up from seeds that had lain dormant all along the shore. In two years' time many had attained a height of six to eight feet, the trunks nearly an inch in diameter.

Pickleweed

Whatever happened to the custom of May baskets? As children we fashioned dozens of baskets from tablet paper or from gaudy wallpaper from the sample book, put them together with flour paste, and filled them with wildflowers —Easter lilies, Johnny-jump-ups, spring beauties, and blue-eyed grass. We hung them on neighbors' doorknobs, shout-ing "May basket for Mary!" (or Alma or Opal or Helen), and ran and hid. Or we left them in rural mailboxes. By the time the flimsy creations were filled, hung, and discov-ered, the contents were withered and drooping. But no matter. The making and the giving filled our hearts with charity. Those baskets *we* received contributed to our feeling of being loved.

Early one afternoon I set out along a path that leads across the saline marsh at the head of Oro Bay, to enter an open wood and follow a fresh-water creek where beavers constructed a dam several years ago. The sharp clean air smelled of new growth. Where salt and fresh water spill over together at extreme flow tide, the earth is carpeted by a thick mat of samphire, a halophyte with jointed, leafless stems, belonging to the goosefoot family.

I could not recall having seen this plant anywhere else on the Island then. I have found it since along muddy banks of other tide creeks, especially along the east shore where flooding is fairly frequent. The odd little flowers, more green than white, arise at the stem joints from a fleshy axis. The entire plant is said to be edible, hence it has come by the name of "pickleweed." I find (with increasing frequency during these nature-awareness times) recipes for making samphire pickles or samphire salad. To me it has a fishy taste.

All of the samphires—indeed all members of the goosefoot, as well as glasswort, families—are lovers of salty bogs. Several are employed as pickle timber. The name "samphire" derives from the French *herbe de St. Pierre,* or St. Peter's herb. For those who might wonder, the plural of goosefoot is not goosefeet but goosefoots. In Britain, members of the family go by such intriguing names as "fat hen" and "Good King Henry," probably for intriguing reasons.

The wood beyond the marsh is an enchanting place at any season. Green frogs leapt from the shelter of pale wet salal leaves. In a clearing made by man and beaver at their work of wood cutting, trout lilies and purple violets bloomed together at the wood's edge. From a clump of wild cherry came the unexpected crow of a pheasant cock. During our first years here, pheasants were fairly numerous in open fields and meadows. We heard the cocks crow often, and saw the drab little hens with their young in the roads and along the fence rows. One summer day a clutch of eleven young birds appeared with a hen underneath the hammock a few feet from the door, to take a dust bath. Grouse, too, in earlier years took advantage of the excellent cover provided by blackberry jungle.

With an increase in both raccoons and hunters, neither of which has a natural enemy here, both pheasants and grouse dwindled to the vanishing point. A few pheasants have been brought in, but these are half-tame birds and do not last long, nor wander far from the release point. The last grouse seen, so far as I know, took up a position each day on a fence post in front of the schoolhouse, from which he attacked passing automobiles, as though in a final gesture against encroaching civilization.

Neither do we see or hear California quail as we did once. For a time last spring I was deceived into thinking I heard quail call, a whistle I find especially musical and appealing. Working in the garden above the cove, I stopped often to listen to a clear, cheerful "way-be-o," repeated at intervals from the vicinity of the gulch. Only after we received as a gift a Roger Tory Peterson recording of songs and calls of western birds did I realize that the lilting three-syllable call, remarkably similar to that of the California quail, was made by Traill's flycatcher, a bird no larger than a good-sized sparrow. By comparing the two as recorded I could finally detect the difference.

I had not visited this woods since the disappearance of the beaver. I found that the careful dam, the tall stick house, had been torn up or washed away. All that remained of the beaver's work were a few weathered alder stumps, chewed to a characteristic point, and scattered sticks that had marked the site of his mostly submerged dwelling place.

Census

*"If only we will let go this idea
that all traffic stops at the
man-made light."*

(JOHN HAY, *In Defense of Nature*)

People I meet these days often ask the question, "How many live on your Island?"

"How many what?" I am inclined to ask sometimes.

Despite our self-esteem, we are only one of the millions of species of fauna. Life here, and elsewhere, went on in quite an orderly manner before our arrival and would, I have no doubt, continue unembarrassed by our departure. Of the wealth of organisms that this small land mass supports, man is in all probability both the least useful and the most dependent.

Were the last human to take his leave, pack up, and set sail for the mainland, never to return again, his absence would scarcely be noted save by his own dogs and cats. Before many years had passed most traces of his handiwork would disappear. His fences and his dwellings would be overrun by growth, his roads largely lost in a march of fir and alder and bracken. After a while, I suppose, the deer would miss his clearings. The raccoons, the birds, the chipmunks would hang about for a time in wait for the largesse of those of us who exchange food for the pleasure of their company. But presumably they too would survive. Among the widely dissimilar organisms, both fauna and flora, that live together in association mutually beneficial, *Homo sapiens,* the single surviving species of the genus *Homo* of the primate family Hominidae, is no doubt the most expendable.

Phyllis

On the first day of May we acquired a slug-eating duck. I had not thought especially of wanting a duck, but here she was, a gift from a friend, a mild-mannered unexcitable bird of a peculiar fawn-red color, with a clipped or sometime broken wing that stuck out at a queer angle. No, he did not know her sex, the donor said, nor had the owner. She might be either.

"She's a she-duck," our next-door neighbor, Murph Bond, who knew about ducks, informed us. "Drakes don't *talk* all the time."

One day we found an egg beside her watering tub, and so we named her Phyllis. She eyed the egg as though surprised by its appearance. So far as I know, she never produced another. We called her "Duck," for short, and she readily responded. I had forgotten how companionable a solitary duck can be. For want of her own species, she became my shadow, following me about on her flat feet, bowing and conversing. Save when the cats approached too close, her voice was dulcet and pleasing. Her reaction to any feline advance was a prolonged hissing that filled the cats with terror.

To please me, I thought, she ate garden slugs by the score. Her own favorite foods seemed to be seaweed, beach grit, fern fronds, the leaves of giant marigolds, and the freshly popped corn Earle provided daily, oiled and salted.

Each evening Duck and I made a trip to the beach, a junket I enjoyed as much as she. Although she was granted complete freedom, she neither visited the beach alone nor departed the back yard, from which she could keep an eye on the door, until along about sunset. Then, she went around to the front to remind me that it was beach time, raised her voice half an octave, and became demanding if

I did not show up soon enough to suit her. Her joy at my appearance was so obvious that I could never bring myself to keep her waiting.

She led the way with loud quacks of rejoicing. We always followed the same routine. I took along a large plastic bag in which to gather seaweed for the compost heap. Because her legs were too short to negotiate the risers of the beach stairs, she employed my shoulder as chariot during the descent.

Deposited beside the water, she waded in, swam, ducked her head, sprinkled and groomed her feathers, then came ashore to burrow in the wet sand with her bill, keeping up a kind of stomp dance accompanied by an ecstatic monologue. Becoming suddenly aware that I had moved along the beach, she would run to catch up, stepping on her own feet with a comical rocking motion. If the tide were high and I was obliged to climb over logs too big for her to negotiate, she took to the water, as graceful as any swan, and swam around in detour.

When I decreed that beachcombing for the evening was over and turned to climb a neighbor's path to the county road, she followed obediently, reliving the evening's fun in soliloquy and pausing here and there to pick up slugs emerged from daytime hiding.

During these excursions the thin line between wild and domestic proved interesting. Wild ducks flying along the beach swept low to look the earthbound over. Appearing to recognize Duck as fellow species, they circled and came back, disregarding my presence. She in turn seemed to acknowledge relationship. Her voice stilled. She tipped her head to one side and cocked an eye to follow the flight. Occasionally she stood high and spread her wings as though she wondered at their lack of function. But as soon as the airborne had satisfied their curiosity and gone on, she resumed her housewifely waddle.

Duck died in August following an attack by a neighbor's

dog. Even now, many months later, the sight of a curled red feather clinging to a fireweed stem or alder branch brings a feeling of loss to which I am embarrassed to confess. She was a faithful companion.

The following spring we replaced her with a pair, a big homely drake whose tail scraped the earth as he walked or ran and a dainty female who bullied him without let-up. Having each other, they accorded us little attention. So far as I know *he* never experienced the joy of salt-water beach. *She* did, once. Cognizant all at once, one evening, of flight function, she arose from the yard, soared over the fence and across the road, and negotiated the high bank, landing in the water, where she was set upon by dogs. Rescued, she paid with a clipped wing and seemed content thereafter.

We lost that pair because of my own negligence. They disappeared one night when I forgot to leave the poultry house door open so that they could go to roost in safety. I remembered about 10:00 P.M., but they were already gone. Although I searched diligently for several hours and for days afterward, I was never able to find so much as a single feather.

More recently a half-wild young pheasant has come to stay with us. Hatched, obviously, as a game bird on a farm at the south end of the Island, she must have wandered away on her own in search of who-knows-what and found herself lost. She feeds peaceably enough among the many songbirds that freeload with us, but remains detached and seems lonely. Each morning she takes up a position on the narrow grassy median between the road and salt water, where she spends the day watching the maneuvering of gulls and ducks, as though she recognized in these larger species a nearer relationship and closer similarity of social behavior.

Merry Month of May

However erratic April's behavior, May is a month to be trusted. To remain indoors for a few days is to fall behind the news. The soft sunlit air was filled with bird song, with feverish and yet stealthy building. Songs, joyous and tender, served as warning. "This is my territory. Keep out. Stay away." Lines are drawn and generally respected. Yarn and ravelings laid out disappear in minutes. A robin braced her feet and pulled at a last year's support string tied to a pole in the pea bed, looking furious and frustrated. A male robin attacked his reflection again and again in a clean-washed hubcap.

Along the trail to the cove, Indian paintbrush came into bloom in orange-red drifts, spilling over the bank to the water's edge. Not having seen the plant elsewhere on the Island, I am inclined to attribute it to Nella Higgins' penchant for scattering wildflower seeds picked up on trips throughout the Northwest. Each year, paintbrush spreads a little farther. A sometimes parasite or semiparasite on the roots of other plants, this *Castilleja* owes its color to scarlet bracts. Flowers are hidden and inconspicuous.

Although various members of the genus (figwort family) begin readily enough from seed, lazy roots go seeking about in the earth until they encounter the root of a suitable host, which they penetrate, stealing a part of their sustenance. Botanists say that this was not always the case with paintbrushes, which number as many as two hundred species, most of them native to North America; that once *Castillejae* of whatever variety were self-reliant. Through successive generations they have formed so firm a habit of dependence that now they can scarcely make it on their own.

From early morning until late evening, violet-green

swallows kept busy at their construction. Seeing one of these alight time after time in tall grass and fly off to the nesting site with a beak full of matter, I went outside to investigate. The mud he was using came from a heap of fresh dog droppings. I recalled seeing various swallows and martins in Kansas collecting nesting material from mounds of cow dung in the pasture, and seeing dry range birds in Texas gathering this only moist substance available.

Throughout days and nights, long beaded catkins from the cottonwood tree rained on the roof, until the eave troughs overflowed and the roof was carpeted from eave to gable. Sticky resinous buds exude a strange perfume. The tree, a loner, never produces the tufts of cotton that choked screens in our Oklahoma house and that are responsible for the name. Like madroñas, the cottonwood is messy by disposition. From the first shedding of catkins and buds to the final fall defoliation that piles yellow leaves knee deep, the amount of litter the tree produces is appalling. Twigs fall throughout the year and the slightest breeze, or nothing at all, may cause a break or fracture sufficient to bring a limb crashing. Underground, hairlike rootlets creep through the smallest crack or crevice and form unsightly masses that block off plumbing drains.

But the tree is a magnificent specimen in any season, dwarfing the tall house to make it look less rangy. In summer the cool heart-shaped leaves whisper together endlessly, and in autumn, before abscission begins, the crown of foliage is a hardly believable translucent gold. "So *yellow* you get lost when you look up," a child of the plains declared.

A three-inch horse chestnut tree, with a pair of opposite leaves made up of radiating leaflets that drooped like the wings of a butterfly at rest, appeared beside the stone-lined fire pit. The parent seed, a shining "buckeye" ejected from a prickly fruit that fell last autumn, lay in the grass, unburied. The single thin stem that bore the leaves emerged from a break in the nut, which was tied to earth by a second hairlike shoot that had gone downward. From the little seed, unplanted, a new and perfect life had emerged. Here was power made visible—aerotropism, the drawing upward, geotropism, the pull downward. How had each infant shoot known the way to go?

One warm evening we sat in darkening woods above the water, concealed by a dense growth of huckleberry and blackcap, and watched and listened to a flock of black brants that had wheeled into the bay to feed and rest during migration. We had seen them come in earlier, flying in a long line over the water, big birds of the goose family, dressed in priestly black with collar of modest white. They kept up a low-voiced conversation, a soft, throaty goose gabble. As they talked they wheeled like a well-schooled drill team, now left, now right, describing curves and circles in the sunset-reddened water. One voice sounded above the others, strident and somehow commanding, as though he called the changes. Even after the night had turned too dark for us to see, the voices and (we presumed) the maneuvering continued.

Broom and Hardhack

By mid-May, the blossoms that had opened on Scotch broom, a naturalized pest from the Mediterranean for which the Scots are blamed, had spread a golden blanket over countless acres in the Pacific Northwest. We do not have a great deal of broom here on the Island. Not enough land has been cleared, and farmers have been ruthless in its extraction, but during a mild year almost any month will see a few of the pea-shaped yellow flowers on sharply angled, nearly leafless stems.

May brings a massed flood. *Cytisus scoparius*, called

"whin" in England, prefers poor soil to rich. When the head of our household flew north and west in May of 1946 to stake out territory, he reported back that Northwest hills carpeted with broom, as seen from the air, resembled "sloping platters of scrambled eggs." On a clear May day, hills across the channel glow a golden yellow. Seen from close up, orange-red stamens produce an odd light.

Grubbed out or burned off, broom comes back tough and resistant, blooms, and sets hairy pods. In the fall the ripened pods burst with popping sounds, hurling prolific seeds like buckshot in every direction, producing a population explosion that outdoes the best efforts of any native flora save the rampant blackberry to thrive and multiply.

Another shrub beginning to bloom in May is hardhack or (more aptly) steeple bush, *Spiraea douglasii,* a pretty, moisture-loving specimen we planted in our gardens in Oklahoma and nurtured tenderly because of the fluffy pink spires of bloom that would appear in summer. Driving west across Montana and northern Idaho in the summer of 1946 on my first trip to the Northwest, I was amazed to see dense clumps and marching lines of this tall shrub we had known as "pink spiraea" growing wild along the draws. Here on the Island I found the same silver-pink steeples arising from wet road ditches and bordering the fresh-water lakes.

They tell an interesting story of an Oregon suburbanite who gave a midwestern mail-order nursery a carte blanche order for suitable shrubs to landscape his newly purchased lots. The shrubs arrived, leafless and carefully packed, and were planted. When spring came and his landscape leafed, he was chagrined to discover that his massed background planting was identical with the wild profusion of shrubs in the fresh-water marsh that bordered the back of his place, a veritable jungle of hardhack, labeled *Spiraea douglasii* on his little tags.

The ditches along and between the bays were a fascinating world in May, a rich mixture of plant and animal life, of dark red salamanders and tiny green frogs, of Mayflies, stoneflies, and green and gold dragonflies. New heads appeared on the tall thin stems of cat-tails, where red-winged blackbirds hung their woven cup nests, and yellow *Mimulus,* bright flowers with monkey faces, sprawled among weak-stemmed brooklime.

In full leaf by May, horsetail forests crowded wet road shoulders along with starry clubs of skunk cabbage like fallen warriors among the yellowing leaves. Fertile fronds of horsetail shook out green pollen. In the small clearings opened by woodcutters, trailing yellow violets, the lower petals pencil-traced with brown lines, bloomed among mats of cool leaves, and sharply angled twigs of red huckleberry, slow to leaf, crossed each other to make a green lattice.

In deeper shade, twinflower extended long thin evergreen arms over moist earth and sent up fragrant pink bells in pairs. Because of their spreading habit of growth, I tended to confuse this green *Linnaea* for a time with the bearberry called kinnikinnick, which prefers drier, more open woods. The flowers of the latter are more urn- than bell-shaped, though similar in color, and appear close to the stem in clusters. Leaves of kinnikinnick, too, are less round and grow *alternately* on the reaching stems. Leaves of *Linnaea,* favorite flower of Linnaeus the namer, have teeth along the upper half of the margin and stand opposite.

Back from the road, kinnikinnick that escaped the poison spray of last summer was hung with pink blooms. The word children like to say is eastern American Indian in origin, credited generally to Algonquin and Ojibwa tribes, and means "that which is mixed." Leaves blended with tobacco were smoked. It is said that Northwest Indians combined the leaves with the inner bark of red osier dogwood, swallowed the smoke, and went into a drunken stupor.

A gentle warm rain washed the landscape. Between showers, a strange association gathered at the feeder—a pair of red-winged blackbirds, purple finches and house finches, white-crowned sparrows, a few swaggering starlings, and a single male brown-headed cowbird. Purple finch males wore crests of maroon velvet. One male house finch boasted a headdress and vest the color of ripe orange skin, or bittersweet berry. This daintier, smaller finch goes by the common name of "linnet."

Song came from everywhere. It was as though each species tried to outdo the other. The purple finch sang alto, sweet and low in pitch. The chirping warble of the linnet was sweet but disconnected. Starlings in spring plumage shone iridescent green and purple, and whistled or grated from the fir bank. Each year they grow more numerous. The cowbird creaked, making a rusty hinge sound. A pair of rufous-sided towhees slipped in and out of the myrtle ground cover, the male black and white and robin-red, his mate in sober sable. They scratch like small hens, sending the dead leaves flying. Towhees have a liking for sprouted peas. They move down the row and mine the wrinkled seeds, leaving the sprouts in a line, like fallen soldiers.

Down by Lyle Carlson's store, serviceberry, an *Amelanchier* of many names, was suddenly clothed from top to bottom with fringed white blossom. Common throughout much of the United States, this shrub with the sweet purple berries goes by the names of shadbush, shadblow, saskatoon, and June berry. Indians mixed the fruit with pounded meat to make a pemmican.

Long yellow catkins on broadleaf maples gave place to winged seeds like small propellers. Alders came alive with bushtits, little acrobatic Paridae that swung back and forth on last year's brown cone clusters and kept up a sibilant lisping. Bushtits flowed in flocks from alder to maple to high fir crowns, mingled with chestnut-backed chickadees, and swept out of sight across the water, weaving in and out like a swarm of honey bees. I found a nest once, a lovely long pouch, in tall ocean spray, and watched the bird come and go. Flocks of bushtits move like blowing leaves in sudden gusts of wind.

In bright sunlight, lupine buds showed purple above silver-green palm-shaped foliage. More than twenty species grow and bloom in Washington. The name "lupine" comes from *lupus,* meaning "wolf." The plant was thought to rob the soil of fertility. Actually, this little pea, as do all the peas, enriches the earth with nitrogen. Leaves fold as though in sleep at night. Flowers that shade from blue to purple with a touch of cream on the petals bloom profusely through June and July and into August. On a meadow slope at Otso Point, lupine spreads a cream and purple blanket. I never see them there but that I remember fields of Texas bluebonnets, another *Lupinus,* like lakes of blue water. In southwestern Oklahoma, wild red and gold gaillardia likewise bloomed in painted pools, the Indian blanket flower.

Sweet-after-Death

In half-shaded clearings, May leaves crowded so thickly together that no earth was visible. These go by the name of vanilla leaf, though no scent is apparent at this stage of growth. Each thin stem held one leaf divided into three segments with scalloped edges, like the wings of big green butterflies. Bruised and trampled plants give off a strong smell of vanilla, or of tonka bean. We bring them home in bunches, hang them up to dry, and presently the entire house is permeated with a fragrance reminiscent of cakes baking. A third name is sweet-after-death.

Before the month was out, spikes of white flowers stood above the leaves on their own wire stems that arise out of earth, having made their way between leaf segments. The flowers do not last long. Petals drop and the stem disappears. The leaves will remain crisp and green until late summer, when they pale, wither, and go over. Then, entire woods will be permeated with the essence of vanilla. Perhaps the aroma has a purpose. It is said to repel flies. Bundles of dying leaves have been used with this in mind, but I cannot vouch for their efficacy. Surely the smell is no kind of lure; it is only present in the dying plant. Why does one mushroom smell of lemon, another of anise, a third of apricot? These are nature's secrets.

Full Summer

Whatever the calendar says of solstice, summer comes full-blown in May. Above feathery leaves of wild bleeding heart, pink pendants hung suspended, each flower a heart-shaped charm. Along the trail to the creek, bleeding heart spreads farther each successive year, mingles with and overshadows the varnished gold of buttercups.

Buttercups are all but universal, and far too numerous and prolific to be choosy. Twenty species grow in Washington alone. They spill out across worn paths and mind not a whit the weight of footsteps. One walks a road paved with burnished petals. All ranunculi have numerous stamens. Some live in water, as the water crowfoot. Petals fall away at a touch. A gold *weed*. But it is a big family, and some members are botanical sophisticates. Monkshood and baneberry are buttercups, as well as pasqueflower, clematis, and larkspur, even blue columbine.

As days lengthened a lull came in bird song. The feeder was deserted save for a few male cowbirds. Females must be staked out, watching. Do they despise themselves? Perhaps I only fancy that the inconspicuous little put-upons have a look of contrived innocence.

Of Owls and Islanders

I suppose you might say I have a thing about owls. They fascinate me. I have replicas, unrealistic but remindful, all over the house, because friends and family know of this somewhat childish aberration. Sometimes a really happy circumstance comes of this.

One evening about nine, Islanders Billy and Harold Hansen stopped in to say that they had seen baby screech owls perched in an alder tree along Lovaas Road at the northwest end of the Island. On the way home they would mark the site. The young would be apt to stay in the vicinity, and perhaps I would see them. I set out early the next morning. I had no difficulty finding the site. An elaborate arrow made of large pebbles had been built squarely in the middle of the little-traveled road, pointing toward a small alder in the edge of the woods. As though instructed to wait for my inspection, two baby owls sat side by side, unblinking.

The arrow remained for weeks, undisturbed by traffic, until the county grader came. Knowing that it represented communication of some sort, Islanders carefully turned out and went around it. A few stopped. At least *one* saw the owls. One of the delightful facets of Island living has been this kind of sharing, only possible in a small community where all of the inhabitants are neighbors, and most appreciate nature in all its facets.

I will venture to say that most Islanders feed wild birds. Several I know feed raccoons. A large part of Lyle Carlson's weekly truckload of supplies from the mainland consists of food for wildlife. An injured wild duck is picked up and cared for. At least one Islander has seen and heard a meadowlark. Three or four have seen the otters. Several have heard a coyote. Someone has discovered a brooding rufous hummingbird. These news items go the rounds, as surely as does the news of human enterprises.

The owls were Kennicott's screech. Other names are "little horned." "mottled owl," "Puget Sound screech." We hear them in the fall, a high-pitched tremolo. The owls are not much afraid. I surprised one once, or he surprised me, when I went into the orchard on a dark night with a flash-lamp to look for a raccoon in the apricot tree. He sat on a low limb within easy reach. Only his head appeared to make a complete rotation as I walked around him for a better look. Although his food consists largely of mice, he is said to attack good-sized birds, such as jays and robins and even full-grown pheasants.

Although I searched diligently, I never found the nest from which the Hansens' owls emerged. Those woods, not often penetrated by man, are filled with snags in which excavations made by woodpeckers are used by owls. Owls nest early and keep their premises clean. In all probability the same cavities would be used over and over again by different species.

And Slugs and Strawberries

Wild strawberries, liking filtered sunlight, bloomed among the new bracken. They never seem to berry here as they did in Kansas. In twenty years I have found no more than a handful of ripe wild strawberries, mostly half slug-eaten. More than any other fruit, they bring nostalgia for past springs. On the slopes of Mount Oread in Lawrence, Kansas, wild strawberries grew to marble size. I wonder how it is now that buildings have multiplied on the campus. Have strawberry beds been obliterated? A dark-eyed girl said, "I wish my breath would *always* smell of wild strawberries."

Slugs are gluttons for strawberries, green or half-ripe,

wild or domestic. They spread slime over the fruit, and glue themselves to the underside of nearby leaves to sleep off their gluttony. Who speaks for the slug? I heard about a child who carries slugs about in little boxes lined with leaves, and swings them in her swing. "Because they're *lonely*. They have no *friends*."

Star flowers hurried into bloom. Held aloft on a long stem above a whorl of leaves, each pale pink corolla appeared to be without flaw, a perfect seven-pointed star. The earth was spread with stars. In deep moist shade star flowers outnumbered trillium, which had lost its pure white look of innocence and turned a pale rose.

Encouraged by eighty-degree warmth, a pair of chipmunks emerged from some underground fortress to engage in a wild game of hide-and-seek among the rocks. A mating game? They look alike. For all they stored last summer, they have a half-starved look. Their coats are rough in early spring. As days warm and mating pursuits begin, they turn sleek and handsome, and their tails fluff out. In this mild climate they do not hibernate for long, some years seemingly not at all. Last year a solitary chipmunk gathered and presumably stored holly berries until Christmas time.

Along the east shore, winter damage from heavy rains and wind-pushed waves gnawed away raw sections of the high pebble-embedded bank. A one-hundred-foot fir tree stood on end, its roots like tentacles, clawing air. Plunging down the steep, the fir had not gone alone. The great tree had taken alder, madroña, and smaller growth, which lay dying on the beach, washed by salt water. All clung to life, but their days were numbered. Would a thousand winters gobble up the entire Island? One old abstract indicates that a shore line has moved back eighty feet in a little more than three-quarters of a century.

True wild blackberries, thorny opportunists, crept over the fallen, flung protective arms across root and bole, decorated the dying with a delicate white flowering. Male and female flowers of blackberries appear on separate plants. Female blooms are smaller and far less in number. Where the crumbling bank still held, thistles had sprung up, fierce armed silver fountains of thin-spined leaves, along with green lupine steeples and shoots of fireweed and foxglove.

A narrow freshet fed by a boggy spring was lined on either side by maidenhair ferns. Delicate fronds hung suspended from shining black crowns bent like hoops or horseshoes. Each subleaflet wore a crown of fringed fronds in overlapping tiers that quivered in air currents created by the energy of falling water. A wren sang, high tinkling trills of sound, and then left off to scold my passage. His nest was somewhere out of sight. He moved beside me as I walked. Sometimes he led, flitting from bush to bush, tail cocked high.

A sudden blaze of orange showed through the trees, a pool of California poppies. How had these escapees come here? I find them in the most unexpected places. They bloom and seed, and seedlings come to bloom and seed, from May throughout the summer. In mild years I find third-generation seedlings blooming in December. Four-petaled flowers unfurl like flags or umbrellas from conical caps that split and fall away. Children like to slip off the caps and see the petals flare before their appointed time, play God in a flower's life.

Seed capsules, too, are cones that split and scatter seeds. Poppies prefer poor soil and sea level, dislike high altitude, and care not a whit for moisture. I have seen them spill in glorious cascades of color down cindered railroad grades. Blossoms close at night and reopen in response to daylight. The root is sleep-inducing and will ease the pain of toothache.

High above salt water the first of the wild roses had opened, pale pink, fragile flowers. At least eight kinds grow and bloom in Washington State, two or three on this Is-

land. Our roses are all equipped with thorns. "Armed,"
the books say. Some are more armed than others.

Wild roses more than any other flower take me back to
Memorial Day in Kansas. We never said "Memorial," we
called it "Decoration Day," and planned for weeks ahead.
My sister Elsie and I went out at sunrise, to comb field and
pasture for wildflowers. Verbenas had gone over, but wild
roses were in bloom, pale pink, delicate, and fragile, and
the cat-claw sensitive briar we called "sensitive rose,"
ground-running, briary plants with rose-pink globose heads.
Bipinnate leaves folded at a touch, intolerant of handling.

We gathered wild roses and filled baskets with rock and
plains larkspur, purple-striped penstemon bells, blue and
cream Baptisia, the coarse, long-rayed, purple-brown heads
of *Echinacea*. We gave the name of "indigo" in error to
bright blue, sticky spiderwort. We wove wreaths from cedar
boughs and from asparagus fern.

The program at the church, of Civil War songs mostly,
was followed by a parade in the hot sun, a procession up
the long hill to the graveyard. (We never said "cemetery.")
As long as he was able to negotiate the hill, Grandpa
Dudgeon marched with the other veterans, a big man in
rusty coat, his white beard blowing back, his broad shoulders proud. We were told that when the war ended and
he was mustered out he walked from Ohio to Iowa to resume his life. The town had one Confederate veteran.
After the ranks were thinned he marched with the rest,
as proud as any. I can see, now, that our history books were
biased.

Behind the wrought-iron fence the dead held open house,
with bright flowers and waving flags. We gathered to pay
tribute to the Unknown Soldier in his small enclosure. My
mind wandered. Who was he? How far from home? He had
been dead for half a century. He would be forever nameless. But the day was pure joy. No one who mattered much
had died, then.

June

The Names and Who They Are

June brought the saxifrages to bloom, the most confusing of all. Mitrewort and bishop's cap are one and the same, *Mitella*, with a capsule shaped like a bishop's mitre. Fringe cup and foam flower, *Tellima* and *Tiarella*, had been in bloom since April. Foam flower is *Tiarella unifoliata*, meaning one leaf to a stem, or *trifoliata*, meaning three. Alumroot bloomed in May. *Tolmiea menziesi*, youth-on-age, is easy. Little new leaves are born in pairs at the bases of old leaf blades.

But I have found foam flower with two leaves to a stem, and capsules of bishop's cap shaped like French berets. Sometimes flowers of youth-on-age are white streaked with green instead of "greenish streaked with purple." Botanists love the word "false" and use it as a red herring. Foam flower is really "false mitrewort."

In a little-used bookcase I came across a yellowed paperback called *How to Know the Wildflowers*, by Alfred Stefferud, an editor of the Yearbook of Agriculture. Mr. Stefferud wrote the book, he explains carefully, for his little daughter, Christine, in response to her modest plea, "I'd just like to know the names of flowers and who they are."

That's all *I* want, and I commend Mr. Stefferud for his efforts in Christine's and my behalf. But I have secret reason to suspect that he, too, was confused about the Saxifragaceae. He gathered alumroot, foam flower, mitre-wort (true, not false) together on a single page. "Alumroots differ in hairiness and the way the leaves are cut," he wrote with fatherly wisdom. "Flowers may be white, pale pink, purple, yellow, or greenish." "Foam flower," he added sagely, "is like them, but prettier."

And so I find it.

Winds of Change

One quiet June morning the sounds of blasting began, and continued intermittently throughout the day. At each explosion the windows rattled and the old house seemed to separate momentarily from its foundation stones, as it does sometimes when the big guns get going at Fort Lewis across the channel. A truckload of logs rumbled past and down the bridge onto the ferry. The Island was enveloped in a haze of creeping smoke. A chain saw whined in the distance.

Distracted by the uproar, I went outside and climbed the hill to the reservoir to check the water level, and then continued along the line fence to look for breaks or downed trees, and out onto the road that runs by the chapel. For some weeks we had seen a small doe browsing on the huckleberry and salal that surround the church parking lot each time we passed, but she was nowhere in evidence. A little way back from the road a bright orange earth-mover was at work clearing for a new road, and I stopped to watch.

Contemporary photographers and artists like to depict these big machines as rearing monsters or sleeping giants, and so they look to me. Like a great broom, the blade swept uprooted stumps, pitted snags, half-decayed logs, and entire live trees toward a smoldering heap over which live flames played and from which blue smoke arose. The road from which I watched was the Ekenstam-Johnson Road, built some time in the 1880s, probably with the aid of oxen. Stumps were grubbed out by hand, or circumvented. The excavation of a single stump was frequently a day's hard work for two men. I could not help wondering what John Ekenstam's or Bengt Johnson's reaction would be to a machine that accomplished weeks of labor in an hour's time. I thought, too, of a recent letter from a retired oil-field worker, in which he applauded the invention of such machines that had freed man from the kind of back-breaking labor that made him old before his time.

From deep in the woods came the thump of a well-driller. Earlier, I had talked with the Island dowser, who lent his psychic services whenever and wherever a well was planned. I have not forgotten the convincing demonstration he gave me once. He had faith in his rod, a hazel withe. He held his arm rigid as he explained the method, and bade me watch closely. The rod began to move suddenly, like a willow pole with a fish on the end. The dowser held his hand steady; only the withe moved in an up and down motion, ten, twenty, thirty times. The magician arose. "There's water at thirty feet, a running stream," he said firmly.

The wind changed. The smoke cleared and blew off across the water. The air smelled of lilacs. In open woods vanilla leaf was white with bloom. A swarm of ants and beetles poured out of decaying logs. Carpenter ant workers are infertile females, the slaves of the species. A snail I found feeding on a leaf resembled, remarkably, the snail

Achatina which I saw by the hundreds in Honolulu. I knew a chill moment of recall. A plague of snails in Florida had resulted from two or three pretty animals brought from the Marshall Islands by a small boy as a present to his grandmother. It is said that a single fertile snail can produce in three years' time a total of eight billion descendants.

By mid-month, orchard and alder trees were defoliated by tent caterpillars. Larvae moved in droves from denuded limbs and twigs to cover blackberry briars, huckleberry, fireweed, a scourge, a pathetic, hungry explosion. We found caterpillars in our food, our beds, and our wearing apparel. Caterpillars came, well-done, from the depths of the clothes dryer. Larvae spread a sheet of plastic over tree trunks. Silken cocoons of encased mummies crowded each other along the house siding, under eaves, and inside the mailbox. A plague. A lesson for man. Hardly crawling room.

Tardy larvae were still seeking pupae space when the first hairy gold-brown moths emerged, creamy borders on their wings, with two diagonal cream lines on forewings. Pretty creatures unless you thought of the egg potential. Presently we found egg cases, varnished bracelets packed with eggs in hundreds, thousands, millions, securely clasping boughs and twigs for overwintering. And so began again the everlasting cycle.

A large urn-shaped nest of bald-faced hornets materialized underneath the eaves outside an upstairs window, a gray Japanese lantern woven from overlapping bands of paper. From behind glass, I watched the nest grow, hoping to see the queen. It is said the queen begins the nest, which may accommodate a family of ten thousand members, the nucleus added to as population increases, an ordered colony of labyrinthine cells. I find the queens' nests, or so I believe, little minature urns no more than an inch or two in diameter, fastened securely to the beams of the poultry house. I bring them in sometimes, but I have never found one occupied.

I regard these social lives with awe and sometimes misplaced pity. They know their places, know how to do their work from built-in knowledge. Each member of the colony is adapted to his own particular job. The unemployed die. The others die when their usefulness to the group is ended. Their jobs are assigned before they are born. The entire life of an individual is ordered for the benefit of all the members. Not one complains. Not one rebels. They live, and die, without reward or praise or punishment.

June Color

Camouflaged among yellow blossoms dripping from the rain tree, laburnum or golden chain, two goldfinches billed each other. The bright yellow male wore a black beret tilted forward. He looked debonair, a gay Lothario. The soft green female made a fine pretense of modesty and shyness. She moved away, but not too far. Her simulated reticence increased his interest, which was probably the way she'd planned it.

The horse chestnut tree came into bloom overnight. Flowers stood up in spires, wine-red or yellow centered, staminate and pistillate blossoms with long projecting style and stigma, and recurved stamens. Bees are guided subtly by spots of color at the base of petals. The English call the tree hyacinth, or "giant's nosegay," "a sight for gods and men." And so it is, a tree to outdo all flowering trees save in the tropics.

A minus-three tide brought to light a kelp crab, *Pugettia*, a little green fellow shaped like a shield. Master at camouflage, or fashion-minded, he had decorated his own carapace with plumes and scarves of seaweed that drifted out behind like a bride's train, or ribbons on a parade float.

I walked along the water's edge and found the beach strewn with excavations left by those who had come and gone. Excavations left open meant death for some, from exposure. Mounds of sand and gravel meant death for other lives by smothering. I found clams with broken shells, the animals left to die. Even a geoduck too small and immature for use had been left lying beside the opened aperture he had occupied as living matter. No boat was in sight, but someone had been there by boat, some thoughtless or ignorant vandal. Who can blame us for posting signs? Not that they do a whit of good.

The shells of mossy chiton are little hammocks lined with turquoise blue and bordered with mossy bristles. The eight curved plates bear delicate tracings on the dorsal side, suggestive of designs used by Northwest Indians in basketwork and sweaters. Patterns in brown, orange, coral, and salmon decorate the shells of clams. A sharp-eyed glaucous-winged gull pecked at a brilliant red sunflower starfish stranded in a tide pool.

Loveliest of all June color comes from the bright orange-red drupes that swing in clusters on wire-thin scarlet stems from long looped boughs of oso-berry, jeweled strands against light green spring growth of feathery evergreens.

The fresh-water creek that negotiates the length of the cove and crosses the shingle carried semitransparent larvae by the thousands, destined to become adults or to be ingested. They all look much alike, shrimp shapes swept inexorably downstream in helpless masses to meet their fate without choice or decision.

I remember a day when my feet, in rubber-soled boots, sank suddenly out of sight in the cove, as though I were being ingested, pulled downward by some giant hand into cold mud. Recalling tales of pedestrians caught in quicksand, I threw myself forward and crept out barefoot on hands and knees to distribute weight. To be buried alive, swallowed by cold mud. A nightmare.

A flock of western tanagers descended into the madroña trees, dislodging creamy urns of blossom, gaudy birds that resemble a band of brightly clothed gypsies. The red-faced males, with swollen beaks, black backs, and yellow breasts and rumps, looked artificial, like birds made up of paper to match a color scheme at a children's party. Females wore greenish yellow. They did not move about as do grosbeaks in migration, but sat and rested, making dry clicking sounds, then swept away all at once, over the beach and above the water, flying swiftly, as though late for an appointment in the Olympics. I was sorry to see them go.

On quiet June days all life seems trusting. A two-point buck deer lifted his head, gave me a curious look from his limpid, long-lashed eyes, and went back to his browse. A goldfinch not three feet away crabbed sidewise up a twig to pick at a holly blossom. I literally turned aside for a purple finch at work disassembling a dandelion seed ball.

A female kinglet, olive gray with a golden crown stripe and no bigger than a bushtit, fidgeted from leaf to leaf in the English walnut tree. She kept up a thin, high-pitched, one-sided conversation. Kinglets build one or two decoy nests as well as the nest put to use, which proves that they are not all nor always trusting. She flipped into the laurustinus, fluttered off to investigate a dogwood leaf, and disappeared into high fir branches.

Cleavers

By the first of June, wild cucumber had sent up stiff stems of white flowers at intervals among big rough-lobed leaves. Long arms of cucumber ran from alder to maple to cherry, clung by curled tendrils, ran on and on in loops, swings, hoops, dropped ten feet to earth, and arose again. The leaves are abrasive, but flowers are delicate. Staminate flowers stand in small starlike clusters. Pistillate flowers, on the same plant, bloom singly, from leaf axils. Later come cunning soft-burred fruits.

Open moist woods were netted with northern bedstraw in flower. This little madder is appropriately called "cleavers." Set with stiff-barbed, retrorse hairs (hairs turned backward, literally), cleavers catches and clings. I went down the slope to check the wild blackberry crop and came back wrapped in madder. Stems are square. Whorled leaves grow in fours like green plus symbols, or sixes or eights, like wheel spokes. Flowers are insignificant, white or faintly pinkish, sometimes fragrant. Stems are weak, resilient, and as crisp as frosted grass. Hence the name bedstraw. Another, daintier bedstraw, with the same symmetry of leaf and flower, blooms all summer.

A flock of band-tailed pigeons winged in to feast on ripened fruit of red-berry elder. Swallows were feeding young. Species band together against marauders. I watched a glossy crow in flight with something lumpy in his beak, pursued by swallows, both violet-green and barn varieties. He looked frantic, dodged this way and that, tried flying lower, tried flying higher. They kept at him out of sight.

One summer a pair of swallows built a nest above the deck of the stand-by ferry *Tahoma* that rarely leaves the

Island slip. Fledglings hatched and feeding began. The regular ferry developed engine trouble, and the *Tahoma* had to go on the run. When the boat set sail with the young aboard, adult birds fluttered and scolded, followed for a distance over the water, came back and flew in circles with distressed cries that brought swallows from everywhere to cry and fly in sympathy.

Some two hours later the ferry returned. The young set up a hungry clamor. Parents worked frantically until the boat pulled out again. Hysterics were repeated, but only among the elders. During crossing after crossing, according to the crew, nothing was heard from the fledglings. Presumably they slept, lulled by the rocking ride. Hearing parent cries as the boat neared the Island shore, they awoke and yelled for food. This routine kept up until the *Tahoma* was berthed as stand-by again. Faced once more by dawn-to-dark labor, one would surmise that the parent birds may have come to regret their return to twenty-four-hour responsibility.

Does began to reappear in the roads and orchards accompanied by their new fawns, speckled, light-footed creatures with soft, innocent, unafraid eyes. They stood still to watch my approach, or came toward me. Once alarmed, or warned somehow by the doe, they bounced away, stiff-legged, like jumping lambs. I saw them in the gulch often, moving along the path or standing beside the creek. They seem to belong there, to be a part of the wild scene. Sunlight filters through boughs and leaves. The air is permeated by a smell of leafmold, wild ginger, licorice fern, the gentle sloping sides hung with ferns. Nothing remains of man's influence save the old hydraulic ram that no longer functions, a few remnants of rotted steps placed there to make the slope easier, and a stump or two with cuts that date back a lifetime. Even the ram was powered by water's natural energy. An observation made by John Muir comes to mind, that man needs places where he can realize that civilization is a thin veneer over the deep evolutionary flow that brought him to his present status.

Meadows

By the end of the first week in June the hay had been cut but not put away. Haying on the Island, the only true crop farming left, grows less each year as livestock dwindles. Meadows go begging. There is something thrifty and traditional about wanting them cut I suppose; all that hay going to waste. The meadow grass, mainly wild, would not go to waste, really, any more than do fallen leaves, bark, trees, or needles. Hay is perishable and enriches earth, whether passed through cow or simply left.

To leave it would benefit such as meadow mice, that build runs, as well as ground-nesting birds and web-spinning spiders. Deer browse in tall grass, unseen, or rest in the sun in flattened round rooms with hay walls. Raccoons beat trails across our meadow to Bonds's blueberry patch. We have no use for hay. Yet each year we contrive to have it cut. We keep a few bales for ourselves, to use as mulch in the garden.

Hearing the mower on the sloping meadow above the house, I wondered whether there might be nests. Our Dad used to pace meadow or alfalfa field before haying began, to mark any bobwhite's nest he found. Protective islands of growth were left. Cottontail rabbits, more expendable, moved from swatch to swatch before the blades as the mower closed in, cutting off escape. As islands of concealment shrank, the rabbits crowded together, were obliged, finally, to flee in terror. This was the moment for which the dogs, the boys waited, the moment of truth, the attempt at getaway. I remember pandemonium. No gun was used, or needed. I remember the excited yipping of the dogs, the rabbit screams. Boys threw themselves bodily on the fleeing animals. This, too, was harvest of a sort. Young rabbit was a staple in our spring diet.

Did I really take part in this mass slaughter? I remember feeling rapport with the animals that I knew had converged in tall hay as the gnashing sickle blades, the heavy-footed horses closed in. But I seem to remember, too, that I shared in the exhilaration that prevailed when the break came. I turned away from the sight of dead rabbits staring and bleeding on the kitchen floor. But that was aftermath. I had been a part of the mob scene that put them there.

Meadows turned silver as haying time approached, and as hay lay in sheets to dry for days afterward. I walked the road at night between Burgs's meadow and the shore underneath a full moon, in an aura and an essence of salt air and new mowing. The entire meadow was flat silver.

Foxglove came into bloom overnight. Lower blossoms were first to open, "dead man's bells," "fairy thimbles," bells with fused petals, pure white, lavender, and rich rose-purple, velvet-speckled in the narrow throat, tunnels for gold and black bees. Each year at Higgins Cove I find a foxglove "sport" or two, a spire with upper terminal flower spread wide like a dancer's skirt. I mark the plants and save the seed, but I am never able to duplicate the mutation.

Along Burgs's fence, hard by the old barn, fireweed opened in magenta masses. Fireweed is *Epilobium augustifolium,* an evening primrose with lance-shaped leaves that flowers in long racemes, a feast of color, a lover of disturbed or burnt-over earth, a healer, the first to cover scars. The plant is said to have risen as though by some kind of miracle to soften the sites of bombed-out London buildings. Like foxglove, fireweed opens slowly from the base of the spire upward. By the time the last flower bursts out of bud, long rose-colored seed pods may decorate the lower portion.

Strangers

One morning I went outside to try to catch a glimpse of the owner of a strange voice that seemed to come from high among the cottonwood leaves. The sound went on and on, with only time for a drawn breath between emissions. I never saw the bird, if bird it was. The tree's crown is rarely without tenants. Small gray-brown pine siskins come in flocks to work the leaves near the top. They look little larger than honey bees, stay but a few minutes, explode all at once, and appear to evaporate.

Woodpecker drillings ring the trunk and limbs; crows, cowbirds, robins, and starlings disappear in numbers, as though absorbed. Red-winged blackbirds yodel out of sight. One night I heard a bickering sound, and stepped outside. Four young raccoons clung to the rough ridged bark. The bickering had not come from them, but from adults somewhere among the foliage. Young raccoons make happy sounds, or they cry like human babies. These did not move. Plastered to the tree, they stared back and down across their shoulders, fluffy balls of fur, blinded and confused by the flash, their eyes bead-bright. They looked like stuffed toys, little Steiff animals designed to resemble raccoons.

A small, bright-yellow flower with long creeping runners and white-woolly, pinnately divided leaves appeared on the saline flat washed by salt water during extreme high, wind-driven tide. A *Potentilla,* called silverweed, it advances over earth baked hard as stone by summer sun. A half-dozen oyster plants, another lover of brackish soil, with purple, many-petaled flowers, came into bloom close by. This one was familiar, a goat's beard salsify we grew in Kansas gardens. We ate the tender stems and roots in a cream sauce and called the plant garden oyster. Grasslike leaves clasp the stem. Another species, *Tragopogon praten-*

sis, is grown as an ornamental and bears yellow flowers. An escapee from Africa and Eurasia, the former is widely cultivated abroad. How had it come here, on this saline flat? Stems and roots are salty. Big spectacular round seed heads form after the flowers are gone.

The sweetest smell of June came from orange honeysuckle that dripped with fragrant bloom, cloyingly sweet, like humans out for favors. I watched a goldfinch swing back and forth on a dangling honeysuckle rope, as though for pleasure in the motion. He took off in roller-coaster flight and called back in four high, sweet syllables.

Most of the birds that sang in May had turned silent. Hummingbird feeders hung untouched except by a notch-eared chipmunk that had somehow learned to suck the tube. His cheeks puffed out like toy balloons. How could he store syrup underground? Earlier, a purple finch took syrup from the tube. Standing on his head, he clutched the slippery glass and thrust his seed-cracking beak into the opening. He is there for moments at a time, having become an addict.

Even the gulls had mostly gone to nesting grounds. The sky over the water seemed empty. One drab female cowbird appeared on the feeding board, flanked by four or five disinterested males. Presumably she had laid her eggs. Who knows how many? Who could guess where? Would she recognize her young when they appeared with duped foster parents? How would they know to join their own species when the time came? Who tells them they are cowbirds? I read about a child who tried, unsuccessfully, to teach a captive cowbird to build its own nest. Above all, who pays for the death of the hapless warbler fledgling thrown from the nest? Who pays for *human* injustice?

The Longest Day

It is said that on the twenty-first of June, the longest day of the year, the festival of the summer solstice, more wildflowers are in bloom than on any other day of the year. My own count on the Island came to ninety. The count could not have been, of course, exhaustive. But it was rewarding.

Wild mock orange, syringa, was in full snowy flower along Ekenstam-Johnson Road in the vicinity of the schoolhouse and in wood margins there. Deer love both bud and leaf. They strip the lower limbs, leave half a leaf here, half a bud there. But the tops of this tall *Philadelphus,* named for an *Egyptian* king, are massed with white sweet-smelling flowers with golden yellow stamens. The air for rods around is perfumed. Straight, reddish stems were once used in the manufacture of arrows, hence "arrow-wood."

For the sake of the perfume I have moved a mock orange close to the back door. Because of the tall doe that comes each night to check the Tropicana and the Cecil Bruner roses for opening buds, I have hung out bags of bloodmeal. Deer react adversely to the smell of blood, even old blood, even blood of another species. So fond are deer of mock orange that Rocky Mountain rangers use closeness of *Philadelphus* browse as another indication of overpopulation of the species in a given area.

Creamy ocean spray is at its peak now. Flowers cascade in long lace panicles over strong-veined leaves. They are well named. I remember a June Sunday when much that grew in the Northwest was still strange to me. We climbed a hill above Hood Canal and looked down on a sea of pink and cream, a vast spread of wild rhododendron and foamy ocean spray.

Small soft snowballs of bloom covered ninebark bushes. I count the shreddy layers that clothe the woody stems but never come up with nine. Green, stemless blossoms soften stinging nettle, but the sting is not lessened. The nettle is thick with bristly unseen hairs, each hair a minute "bottle" that pierces the skin and breaks, to release a burning load of acidulous fluid. But the plant is useful, edible in a young stage, and fibers have been used in spinning and weaving. The word "needle" is said to have given rise to the word "nettle." Samuel Pepys in his diary (1661) told of eating nettle porridge. During the Second World War large quantities of nettles were gathered in Britain and the chlorophyll in them extracted for use in medicines and to make a green dye used in camouflage.

July

Pollution

We have come to expect the month of July to be a time of ripening and fulfillment. As though by some internal miracle, orchard trees had recovered from defoliation and had set fruit, however scanty. The earth no longer crawled with caterpillars or swarmed with moths. We were not deceived, but at least we were not reminded.

Evergreen huckleberry, red and tender with new growth in May, had hardened to shining green, and thick clusters of berries had set and commenced to turn color. Salal and mahonia were in fruit, and berries hung thick and ripe on trailing wild blackberry. Scattered areas of ripeness appeared on Himalaya and evergreen escapees along the roadside.

Wooded Guthrie Road was warm with filtered sunlight. For several days a haze, half smoke and strange for summer, had reddened the sun's rays and lain low over the water. Some whim of atmosphere, of wind or barometric pressure, had brought industrial smog from the cities of Tacoma and Seattle. The air felt thick and weighted, and smelled of sulphur. But then to our immense relief the cloud was swept away overnight. Stars and sun shone clear. We could see the mountains, even Glacier Peak, more than half-way to the Canadian border.

Clean air that morning seemed a special favor. I had turned into Guthrie Road on the way home from the store. The woods on either side of the road are lovely at whatever season. But something was wrong. No rain had fallen, yet shrubs and overhanging boughs were glistening wet, and the air smelled noxious. When I had topped the rise I could see a slow-moving truck ahead. Men armed with hoses were drenching roadside growth with a steady fountain of some chemical solution. Unable to pass, I fell back.

The morning was quiet, with little wind, a fortuitous time for spraying, but I was puzzled as to objective. No telephone wires ran here, no electric lines. No project, such as widening, was being undertaken. Most of the shrubs being sprayed—huckleberry (both red and black), Oregon grape, salal, elder, blackberry, and blackcap—hung heavy with fruit that would serve through fall and winter as food for a variety of wildlife. Walking the road the day previous, I had encountered two children with buckets, gathering and eating blackcaps.

The rig moved into the open and began the descent. The silver spray, aimed high, swept taller Himalaya, thimbleberry and honeysuckle, wild cucumber and madroña, drifted across purple lupine in a misty cloud, and drenched fireweed, wild rose, and foxglove that swarmed with bees. A robin that had stood his ground flew away, his feathers sopping wet. A bedraggled butterfly crept across a wet leaf of coltsfoot.

For days the evil smell persisted in the narrow, closed-in road. By the end of the month the dead and dying lined the roadsides. Summer had given way to winter. Plumes of ocean spray, pinkening spires of hardhack, and crisp foliage of *Philadelphus* turned black along other roads. Exhausted-looking cucumber and honeysuckle vines festooned defoliated alder seedlings, dogwood, vine maple, snow- and thimbleberry. Once-green fronds of sword fern and bracken turned a sickly beige. Kinnikinnick on banked road shoulders was a mass of dead stems. Among autumn-brown leaves, wild blackberries hung in aborted clusters.

Some of us dispatched a letter of protest, but no answer came. To us, the spraying made little sense. Some said vaguely that perhaps it made for better traffic vision, pointing to blind corners, and remarked that at least it killed the nettle. But spraying had followed open roads where no nettle was in evidence, roads lined with snowberry and wild rose. We heard that the work bill had run well into three figures, a sum that surely would have covered a good deal of ax and saw clearing where this was needed.

The smell went away gradually. But the character of many of the roads had changed. Nature did her utmost. Rain came and washed the leprous-looking foliage. By the following spring new growth had only partially clothed bare woody skeletons. Sword ferns thrust through dead bracken. In some spots where such had not been seen, opportunist nettle and thistle sprang up green and strong. Sorrel and plantain replaced kinnikinnick and twinflower. Long arms of trailing blackberries emerged from roots beyond the poison line.

Perhaps no real harm was done. Some trees and shrubs died from the defoliation. Much dead wood remains on lower portions of other trees. Whether wildlife left the poisoned fruit alone or whether there was loss from that we have no way of knowing. We warned the children but had to let the birds and animals go. A year, two years later, the feeling and the smell of richness still seemed somehow diminished and diluted.

I do not blame the men who sprayed; they had their orders. And most of us stand guilty somewhere. There is that about a spray in hand, a panacea under pressure. We overuse. Like a child with a squirt gun, we press the button until the liquid is exhausted. For my own part, I confess to a sense of guilt concerning slugs and snakes, or at least an uncomfortable suspicion. Following the acquisition of Duck, I had stopped the use of slug bait, for her sake. I know the bait had been effective. I found heaps of slugs reduced to slime and live slugs feeding on cadavers and likewise dying. The slugs were expendable enough. But I cannot erase from my memory (or my conscience) the sight of a dying grass snake I found beside the fence. Underneath a mat of spice pinks I found another, too sluggish to attempt escape. He, too, died. These were the last snakes I have seen on this place, where snakes were numerous when we first came. Have I inadvertently launched my own lethal chain—bait, slug, snake? And what of the little accipiter I saw struggling away over the trees to her fledglings with a snake in her beak?

The Quiet Time

Of weekday evenings after the last ferry has sailed for the mainland a special quiet settles over the Island like a blessing. The beach is deserted, and roads are bare of traffic. No sound of saw or tractor breaks the stillness, only the gentle lap of tardy water from the ferry wake, the distant rumble of a train three miles away along the mainland shore, the chirp of a chipmunk, the cry of a killdeer. By

July most gulls have long since gone to nesting grounds.

Darkness is a long time in coming. Even at ten o'clock and after, Mount Rainier still holds a blush of coral, the buff buildings on McNeil a wash of late sunlight. After the wake subsides, still water mirrors pink clouds, the first stars to wish on. Cool sweet air smells of iodine.

Hedged in by quiet water, backed by high bank, I like to sit and look out, or walk the beach. By early July, bitter cherry had set stingy fruits. Broadleaf maples were hung thickly with winged samara among five-lobed leaves a foot or more across, wings that hung in clusters, half folded, like swarms of big green moths or butterflies. These maples supported gardens of licorice fern that fringed the upper limbs and cascaded down moss-covered trunks.

All growth appears to love salt air. Flower colors along the shore seem brighter and whites seem whiter. Big snowy thimbleberry flowers stood out against broad, lobed, locked-together leaves. Among the blossoms, early flat fruits were already reddening. Salmonberries offered scarlet, haired fruits. Wild roses bloomed a deeper pink, lupine a richer purple, fireweed a more intense rose. Foxglove was royal velvet.

Plumes and tassels of goatsbeard dripped rich cream. Not a true shrub but a herbaceous perennial, goatsbeard dies down each year. The name comes from drooping panicles that hang from ribbed stems among sharply serrate leaflets. Tiny flowers hang in strings like beaded portieres. Each year a specimen of goatsbeard comes up faithfully beside a red-berry elder against the red-painted poultry house. Both plants are wild. When the elder is in berry the goatsbeard is in flower.

In July the east bank along Yoman Point is like a flower show, with tier upon tier of bloom. Spring flowers have waited for summer flowers. The only spray here is salt spray. The bank is thick with alumroot. The sun is gone finally. The water turns from pink to gray. Far back along the beach a mother raccoon emerges with her fat young and makes her way down to water. Like fur balls, the young roll after. I would like to watch, but these are nocturnal people with sight adapted to their needs. Deer will be down presently, and bats, and owls perhaps. I have no business here, and it has grown too dark for *me* to see.

New Generation

Striped pine siskins with notched tails and yellow wing bars worked the pines from top to bottom, moving from branch to branch and from cone to cone, keeping up a "t-t-t" like first graders saying phonics. Obedient to some signal unheard or unseen by me, they flew from tree to tree all at once, to land like a tossed net among the foliage.

Purple finches came in families to the feeder and ate peacefully together. Parent birds stuffed the heavily striped young with chick scratch. Save for the clamoring mouth, child and mother are look-alikes. A brown-striped sparrow without a tail came. Thinking that the cat had de-tailed him, I brought the cat inside. But then another "bunty" came, and another. Field guides show thirty-two sparrows but not one without a tail.

The young of swallows tried flight and lined the wires. Hummingbird young came in droves, swarming around the feeder tubes and engaging in fierce stabbing battles. Their throats were broadly freckled. Adult males were suddenly back. Where had they gone during nesting, and why? Some say they go to spare the food supply for their families. Others say they leave because their bright colors might betray the location of the nest, that later in the year they return a second time to lead the tribe south.

Killdeer appeared on the beach with young. A family of great blue herons circled above Oro Bay woods, their long legs trailing. They all looked the same size. Blue herons remain in the nest until fully grown and ready for flight. It is said the young are pushed out, then, as are young domestic pigeons. "Fly or fall."

More fawns appeared in the roads. This seemed a year for twins. When we saw one fawn emerge, we waited for a second. One night a doe came down the road with three identical young no larger than jackrabbits. *She* leapt into the roadside growth, but the young came toward me three-abreast, then turned and bounced away in step, as though they heard a polka. They seemed scarcely to touch earth.

It is said that deer herds handle their own density problems. When they become too numerous, does fail to breed or fawns die young. When numbers fall off, does produce twins or triplets, and fawns are stronger. On government-controlled McNeil Island, around seventy-five deer are killed each year, to keep the herd in balance. But deer swim, too, from Island to mainland. One day we watched a doe through the glasses. She had gone into the water below Amsterdam Bay, possibly chased by dogs. Periodically all motion would stop, and we could barely see her head, as though she floated or trod water. But presently she would set forth as though with renewed vigor. We saw her leave the water and deliberately enter woods back from Devil's Head. Once, an Island neighbor in an outboard encountered an elderly buck deer that seemed to be in difficulty. Cutting his motor, the Islander approached the swimming animal, grasped the rack of horns, and towed the animal to safety.

Forerunner of Autumn

Wherever earth along roadsides had been disturbed by plow or scraper, shabby tufts of field chamomile, nondescript daisy flowers with yellow centers and frowsy shredded leaves, formed a solid border. This tousled flower with a disagreeable odor also answers to the names of "dog fennel" and "stinking Mayweed." An herbalist named Gerard referred to the smell as "naughty."

Having read in English fiction, especially children's fiction, of "chamomile tea," a brew said to engender patience, I researched the plant. The chamomile from which tea is made is *Anthemis nobilis*, a fragrant cousin. Ours is *Anthemis arvensis*. In disturbed sour soil *arvensis* associates with *Polygonum*, a smartweed with knotted joints, and the red seed tops of sorrel. I confess to a liking for the *Polygona*, which grow worldwide. Sharply angled, with swollen arthritic-looking joints, they bear little bottle-brush flowers in white or rose. The one called water buckwheat, or lady's thumb, grows half-submerged in lake and pond, the pink flowers afloat. When the swamp dries up in summer, lady's thumb covers cracked and hardened mud like a bright pink carpet.

The Lambert cherry tree, in full ripe fruit, swarmed with cedar waxwings. Their waxed wing coverts shone red-gold. They moved from limb to limb, tasting and testing. It is said that waxwings will pass a fruit from bird to bird in well-mannered sharing. I have not seen this. A stolid robin sat and gorged himself without moving. A woman I know destroyed dozens of waxwings with a pellet gun because of the fruit they consumed, but a tree filled with waxwings is a feast for the eye. I once knew a woman who hated and feared *all* birds in the belief that they carried lice.

Skies remained cloudless, and time stood still of afternoons. Dust veiled the growth along the roadsides, and woods took on a dry look. We read of "closed" areas, of forest fires, and felt uneasy. We have not had a major fire in my time here.

Bright orange tiger lilies with flame-colored recurved petals came into bloom in scattered places. Their nodding freckled flowers with long drooping anthers opened above whorled lower leaves. Corollas ranged in color from the shade of Arizona orange skin to deep rust red. Pearly everlasting produced clusters of silver balls with yellow bead centers embraced by papery scales.

The smell of dry ripe grasses more than any other fragrance brings memories of Kansas childhood—the smell of chaff, rosin, ragweed, and bittersweet along the fence rows. By the last of July the only color left on the lawn was that of hairy cat's ear, bright yellow composites on long green stems above rosettes of hairy leaves, persistent weeds to grownups, flowers to children. A weed, said Emerson, is a plant whose virtues have not been discovered. What is a worthless person?

We scanned the sky for clouds, and turned pages and switched knobs in search of rain. The water in the reservoir dropped to an alarming level. Even of nights, slugs kept to dark places where a trace of moisture held. Most garden plants withered and drooped. I made lists of drouth-resistant species to plant another year—ageratum and nasturtium, gold and brown rudbeckia, California poppies, all the daisies.

Of evenings the few remaining gulls clustered along the tide line in company with flocks of sand "peeps" little larger than sparrows. The sandpeeps were restive, took off, flew close to water, and changed and banked in intricate maneuvers. On the beach they dashed forward, making quick teetering stops. They look like small hump-shouldered gnomes. They bobbed their heads and kept up a plaintive peeping.

On a Sunday afternoon we heard oddly human crying sounds that seemed to come from underneath the ledge of a high bank formed by the crumbling away of earth around the roots of maple and madroña. Presently a baby raccoon emerged and peered out from a tangle of honeysuckle and huckleberry. Throughout our picnic supper he watched us, bright button-eyed, from between the rails of the cedar fence, but he declined to come closer or to accept our offerings. When we approached too close, he retreated. We heaped leftovers beside the fence. In the morning the last crumb was gone.

St. Johnswort, introduced from Europe, appears in increasing amounts each year. Pretty weeds, with golden, black-dotted petals and protruding yellow stamens that give the flowers a feathery look, the plant is poisonous, but only to light-skinned animals. In the Old World, these flowers were said to open on June 24, St. John the Baptist's day. Hung at doors and windows on St. John's Eve, they were thought to be a safeguard against approaching evil spirits, balm for a warrior's wound, and a cure for melancholia.

July is an anniversary of sorts. This coming July we will have lived in Puget Sound country a quarter of a century. This is *home* country. But sometimes a sound or fragrance will trigger a flood of memories . . . the glint of fireflies of summer evenings; the monotonous sleepy chirp of an unseen cricket; the night song of a mockingbird or the lament of a whippoorwill, the fiddling of a katydid. And, oh, the shrilling of cicadas in the elms!

On an evening in July last summer we watched and listened to a nighthawk, a childhood favorite. As children we called him "bullbat." Some call him "nightjar." At dusk you can see the white spots underneath his long pointed wings. He climbs the air with a nasal "pee-nt, pee-nt," lonely interrupted cries followed after an interval by a whirring sound probably made by wing feathers, an explosive boom as brakes are applied. A remarkable as well as useful bird, he flies with mouth gaping, scoops up insects, mosquitoes, termites. As many as a thousand insects have been found in a nighthawk stomach.

Neither hawk nor bat, the nighthawk is a nocturnal bird, cousin to the whippoorwill. Formerly, the birds were said to suck the milk of goats. *Chordeiles,* of the order Caprimulgiformes, family Caprimulgidae, he has a large flat head, an enormous mouth for his size, and does not see well in daylight. I have seen a few by day. Perched lengthwise on a limb, eyes half-closed, they are difficult to spot.

An evening or two later we experienced the wonder of aurora borealis, the northern lights. We had seen the lights a few times as children. At least we had witnessed faintly rosy flashes similar to sheet lightning in the northern sky that our Dad told us were northern lights. But these were the real thing, the big show, the center ring. This was silent cinerama. We did not merely watch; we were embraced, involved, engulfed in moving, vivid color. Long flashing streamers draped the sky, converged in an arch overhead, changed constantly, showing luminous waving bands of rose, red, gold, gray, violet, flame, yellow-green, folded and fluted. You half expected to hear the voice of God, to see the gauze curtains swept aside, the sky open. It was like a divine portent, the end of the world, a delirious nightmare. I stood speechless, covered with gooseflesh. And then the colors wavered away, fading to a pale gray-rose. The sky turned black, and stars came out. The show was over.

Dodder

Dry weather prevailed, and the Island swarmed with visitors. For the first time we saw camper trucks along the roads of nights. Bays filled up with boats on Friday evening and rolled out like tidewater late on Sunday. With the advent of a few miles of all-weather roads, motorized cycles invaded.

An orange net appeared on matted samphire on marshy ground at the head of Oro Bay. Brilliant threads crossed and recrossed, and made an abstract design that spread in all directions, a disordered silken web of parasitic dodder.

Dodder, a *Cuscuta* (strangle-weed, gold thread, devil's hair, hell-bind), begins as an independent. Leafless save for rudimentary scales, devoid of chlorophyll, provided with sucking organs called *haustoria*, this strange plant begins as a thread attached to earth and swings out in a circle, counter-clockwise, searching for a host.

Cuscuta salina, a lover of salt, this one found a salty host in pickleweed or samphire (*Salicornia* spp.). And so began a union that, carried far enough, could only terminate in death for both. Having discovered a host, dodder fuses tissues with her fleshy partner, a fatal marriage. Finally, both plants take on an ashen color. This untidy love vine comes in 170 varieties and attacks various species. It bears strange small flowers and sets abundant seeds. In some states it is prohibited by law. In one plains state, more than one dodder seed in five grams of lespedeza seed has brought penalties to seed sellers.

Magenta Month

July was magenta, a month of warm color. The word "magenta" means rose-purple and comes from Magenta, a town in northern Italy where French and Sardinians defeated Austrians in 1859. A rose-purple town? Massed flowering of unscented perennial peas, a mixed-up wild and garden variety of *Lathyrus,* blanketed shrubs and fences in a weak-stemmed sprawl, in long ridges of color. Drooping clusters of big keeled flowers covered climbing tendrils.

Like human hair, petals and keels of everlasting peas turn gray with age. Hairy pods set, ripen, split, and shoot their seeds in prodigality. Each year the plants grow more numerous. They die down in autumn, but come up rampant in spring.

The modest heal-all is another July flower, but not exclusively so nor always rose-purple. Heal-all, or self-heal, *Prunella vulgaris,* is sometimes royal purple, even bright blue, but usually magenta. Petals are as soft to the touch as fur or velvet cloth. I have found the flower as early as May and as late as December. Once in January I found a bright magenta heal-all standing above the snow on a road shoulder. It comes by its name honestly. When quinsy was popular, before tonsillitis was invented, heal-all provided a panacea. Modern-day Indians use the plant to treat boils. "No one who keeps *Prunella* needs a surgeon," Jean de la Ruelle, physician to Francis I, wrote as early as the sixteenth century. Scattered, and in poor soil, heal-all escapes notice. It has a weedy look. But on a sandy moist slope above Yoman Point this little mint appears each year in such numbers and of such clear color as to resemble an embroidered tapestry or a French mosaic.

Rose-purple asters began to show, and rose-purple thistles, and wild geranium. Hedge nettle—coarse, weedy, and evil smelling—opened whorls of lipped, rose-purple, trumpet-shaped blossoms. Throughout the long days, band-tailed pigeons feasted on ripened fruits of rose-red elderberries.

At ten o'clock one evening we watched a flycatcher, genus *Empidonax,* species unknown (to me), work in silence from his home base on a limb of the Gravenstein apple tree. Like a rubber ball attached by elastic to a paddle, he was launched out, pulled back, time after time, to the identical spot. His tail went up and down like a pump handle. Did he have a crest or merely a bump on his head? Was he Traill's or Alder? Books say call notes are useful in sorting this full field of flycatchers. Helpful examples given are "tosweek . . . preet . . . reek . . . wheech . . . rrrynk . . . week tse weer . . . reek rair . . . whitchy koo . . . prets kew . . ." or simply, "a whistle superimposed on a buzz." This one worked in silence.

A tiger swallowtail butterfly contested with a rufous hummingbird over a stalk of red hot poker, a gaudy cluster of tubes filled with nectar. The butterfly came off battle-scarred, a square of wing and half a tailpiece missing. Unarmed, defenseless, no longer glorious, he sideslipped and crash landed. The rufous sipped and zoomed away, uncaring.

Day of the Whales

One late afternoon a pod of killer whales passed, having detoured deep into Puget Sound presumably during their annual migration down the coast. We stood on shore to watch and listen. The big dolphins dived and surfaced, spouted and sounded. White markings showed brilliant white against blue-black, wet bodies in the deep blue water.

Beaked snouts broke the surface. The sound came like the shot of a pistol or the crack of a rifle. These were "small" whales, no more than twenty feet in length, toothed, and supposedly fierce, said to attack giant toothless whales and to be true killers.

The pod moved slowly. Unwilling to give them up, we sped across the Island when they had passed from view, to watch them pass Otso Point, a Macy parade of incredible mammals like inflated balloons. As do overweight swimmers, they have a buoyant, weightless look in water and move with a lovely ponderous grace that commands respect and awe.

Farther north, ingenious traps have been set to capture these giants for show, and several have died of injuries.

It is said that whales are a throwback to land mammals, a reversal in evolution. Front legs have become flippers, and hind legs are lost. The tail is made up of horizontal flukes. Long after they had gone from sight beyond Devil's Head, we could hear the explosive soundings.

We watched for their return. The Island lies in a pocket at the extreme end of inner Sound; they would be obliged to pass again on their way out. Perhaps they went out by night, or slipped through Pitt Passage. We watched for days but neither saw nor heard them.

August

Dipper

The dipper is a comparative newcomer at the cove. Ornithologist E. A. Kitchin, who marked Anderson Island birds for me in his *Distributional Check-List of the Birds of the State of Washington,* does not list this water ouzel, *Cinclus mexicanus,* as Island resident or visitor. Obviously he never saw one here. Nor did we until recently.

A stubby-tailed bird, the dipper resembles an oversize wren, in old-fashioned, erased (but not washed) black-board color. He honors the cove by his presence. You can't watch him without a smile. He is well-named, dipper. He stands and curtsies at the water's edge. A solitary bird with special oil glands, he wades in, goes over his depth, swims, or walks about on the bottom, feeding. Fish eggs are a favorite food. His occasional song is clear, liquid, and ringing. Preferring turbulent streams, he builds his nest from moss, with a side door, frequently behind a waterfall. The little creek that crosses the cove has no suitable nesting site, so perhaps he comes only to feed.

I saw my first dipper in the fast-flowing Animos River during a visit to Durango, Colorado, in the Rocky Mountains. Dipping and bobbing, he stood on a rock in the midst of white-foaming rapids, a small wrenlike stranger with short up-thrust tail. As we watched with disbelief, he stepped into the water and disappeared from sight. Moments later, this incredible bird emerged downstream with apparently dry feathers, fluttered to a position on another rock, and resumed his curtsying.

It was several years before I saw another, on Mount Tahoma Creek on the high slopes of Mount Rainier, during a blueberry gathering expedition with our son and his family. I still remember the gusts of laughter and gasps of astonishment on the part of granddaughters Lael and Hollie.

Last summer, two small cruisers rounded the sand spit at high tide and entered the quiet cove. The kingfisher rattled an alarm. A great blue heron arose from a perch beside his nest. A pigeon guillemot with bright red legs exploded from a hole in the bank of diatomaceous earth and headed across the water toward Filuce Bay on the peninsula. The water ouzel fled upstream.

The entrance to the cove is narrow, partially closed now by fallen trees. The boats, one behind the other, were barely able to squeeze through the passage. Beer cans and other debris went overside and floated. Double wakes of blue-green oil followed gurgling outboard motors.

The cove belongs to the kingfisher, the heron, the ouzel, the guillemots. And so we ventured a courteous protest. We received our answer. "But you don't own the *water*." And so we don't.

The In-between

Take most years, and August is a strange month, a maverick on the calendar. Neither altogether summer nor yet quite autumn, she lies somewhere in a void between. This year was no exception. A haze, neither cloud nor fog, filtered the sunlight. Smoke trembled along a blue horizon and dust raised by passing cars coated the growth along the roadsides. June had shown us all the blues, sky and flowering and water, and autumn after rain would don her usual golden mantle. But August flowers along the road borders had a dusty, faded look. Purple and rose had grayed, and whites had lost their clarity. Yarrow and pearly everlasting looked merely soiled.

By August the bright new foliage on huckleberry and fir had hardened and darkened, and the summer's crop of insects had done their work of gnawing, nibbling, and boring. Pupae had been mostly spun and eggs laid for overwintering. Seed parachutes filled the air and settled over leaf and petal; cucumber and honeysuckle looked exhausted. On cloudy days a chill arose from both earth and water. There ought to be a *fifth* season named August.

During twenty years of wandering I have not yet walked all the Island trails. Some, made long ago by woodcutters, simply peter out, end abruptly and come up sharp against scarcely penetrable nettle, thistle, blackcap, or gummy gooseberry with long thick spines. Or a path may begin and end for no apparent reason.

I left my trench shovel beside a crumbling log and followed a faint path, which unexplainably widened. The road climbed gently and as gently began descent. Sword fern with six-foot fronds lined the sides, and bracken fern stood head-high in the median. A western hemlock towered almost out of sight, surely a virgin tree. Fir, cedar, alder, and maple trees had reached awesome proportions. How much longer could such a wood remain intact?

A great warm room materialized, a druids' convention hall open to the sky. A fir had gone down, taking with it a dozen lesser trees and leaving a clearing. Flowers of ocean spray had turned to brown husks around the edges, as had the creamy tips of mountain balm. Leaves of mountain balm had rolled because of dry weather and presented a velvet undersurface, a strange shrub that would seem to belong to a desert climate. The air had a pungent smell from this laurel and from the drifts of yarrow, an astringent weed, *Achillea millefolium*. Achilles is said to have used such a plant to cure the wounds of his soldiers. Deer and all manner of insects leave the plant alone. Ferny leaves, from which comes the species name of *millefolium* (a thousand leaves), give off a sickroom smell, an odor of disinfectant. Some flowers have a pinkish cast, but most are soiled white.

Yarrow is nearly universal. The English people formerly used it as a tonic, to stanch blood and to cure colds. Northwest Indians still use it widely, for a variety of ailments. As a last resort, when pastures dry, cattle eat the plant. Milk and butter produced by yarrow-eating cows smell and taste like disinfectant.

Opportunist Himalaya briars were hung with shining clusters of berries as large as robins' eggs. Thistles stood head-high, topped by plumes of seeds like white, uncombed hair. A few purple asters were coming into bloom, not really purple, but a pale washed lavender. One wore a Monarch butterfly, a perfect specimen, bright orange with a black and white border.

End of Drouth

A gentle rain fell in the night, and we awoke to a world washed clean of dust, an August world with a smell of spring. This is not the same as the rain smell we experienced in the Southwest. I have never been able to describe this, nor have I seen an attempt at explanation. Approaching rain announced its coming there with advance aroma (as did snow and hail). The first drops gave off an unforgettable fragrance. Oncoming wind or hail smelled of sulphur. "If the essence of rain could be distilled," a Southwest friend remarked, "what a marvelous perfume!"

A clean wind blew pearl-gray clouds across the sky, and steel-blue water was dotted with the tossed white manes of running whitecaps. Sparrows and finches scorned the birdbath and bathed in wet grass. The word "drouth" is a joke of course, a misnomer here. No one suffers. Nothing dies. Grass greens in a week following the first rain. How would one describe to a native Puget Sounder who had not experienced them the searing winds of Oklahoma, Kansas, and Texas, burned cornfields that rattle like blown wrapping paper, stunted crops, and drouth-exhausted people? Gardens in the dust bowl planted one spring came up the second, then died for want of moisture.

We stopped along a road once during horse-and-buggy days, I remember, to ask for a cup of water. The landscape was burned to a brown crisp, and no sign of green was visible. "This year I planted broomcorn," the tired farmer joked. "All I raised was handles."

Coming to the Northwest, we soon forgot heat and dryness, and took climate for granted. We complain of the rain when we ought to sing hosannas.

Robins brought off a second brood hardly discernible from the first, which still wore speckled stomachers. I fancied the mother robins showed less enthusiasm for the second hatch. But food was plentiful after rain. Earthworms arose to the surface, lay drowned on sidewalks, and were consumed by hundreds. I discovered, accidentally, when I poured chlorine bleach on a bit of earth that chlorine brings dead angleworms to the surface. I felt like a murderer.

Big, clean, sugar-sweet blackberries hung thick and ripe on the Himalayas along the back of the long poultry house. Beaten paths of raccoons and deer make convenient cul-de-sacs where I can stand and fill a bowl for breakfast. Blackberries in a bowl, dyeing sugar and milk deep pink, remind me of Kansas dewberries. A deserted hummingbird's nest hung at the end of a briar, where any breeze must have rocked the fledglings. Barn swallows that nest on crossbeams of the poultry house passed unerringly in and out through wire meshes. The blackened chimney that went down one frightening morning during a fire lies where it fell, a mute reminder.

Sea Harvest

Each morning the beach was piled with red and green algae. Algae lay in windrows at low tide as though raked by a giant reaper. Some leaves were perforated. Long brown crinkled streamers terminated in many-fingered holdfasts clasped tight on less than fist-sized pebbles, like hands that have picked up rocks to throw. Lovely ten-foot leather ribbons of brown kelp streamed out from bulbs that popped underfoot. Slimy green masses without form lay in wet heaps. A mat of algae as wide across as a room and a foot in thickness had turned white. Branched rock-weeds clung to boulders higher up.

My favorite was made up of red-brown silky threads, woven to form a net. A species with ruffled red blade was remindful of the "jabots" my mother wore. The name of the weed is red jabot laver. Some change color quickly when taken from the water. One feathery red algae wore tips like tiny claws. Another resembled yellow-green silk floss used in embroidery.

I brought up one of each, spread them on a table, got out my seaweed books, and tried to identify them. But my list was filled with question marks. Blister rack? Desmerestia? Agarum? Nearly all had air bladders. "West coast kelps are larger and more imposing; some grow to lengths of over 100 feet." Nereocystis? Macrocystis?

When the water cleared I stood on the ferry bridge and looked down into a veritable underwater forest of brown "trees" that waved and swayed with moving currents, a drowned jungle, a "Sargasso sea." But sargassum weed only grows in tropical waters.

Late Flowering

Tardy blue-berry elder came into bloom, big flat creamy flower heads that seemed to change overnight to fruit clusters of soft blue tinged with a lighter blue "bloom" the color of skimmed milk. By the last of August, Pacific dogwood had passed into a second flowering among clusters of red berries. Strong-veined leaves had colored rose-wine. The trees were like fruit and flower bouquets shaken by feasting robins.

Band-tailed pigeons fed on dogwood and alder, and came but rarely to the grain on the feeder. Their preference is for fruit, and they move from Island to mainland and back again as various fruits ripen, feeding by turns on wild bitter cherry, blackberries, dogwood, elder, huckleberry, cascara, salal, and mahonia, fruits-of-the-month for pigeons. Ornamental fruits consumed include hawthorn and fire-thorn, holly, mountain ash, and the many berried cotone-asters. A favorite game bird, these swift fliers have their own methods for survival. Flocks remain small and scatter widely. Only one or two white eggs are laid per season, in an untidy platform nest built of sticks high in a coni-fer. Infrequently vocal, they sound more like owls than pigeons.

Heavily built birds, dove-shaped and of a soft rose color, band-tails have small heads and yellow feet and bills. The name derives from a broad, light gray tail band set off by a black stripe. A second name, "white-collared pigeon," results from a narrow white strip across the nape of the neck. The range of the band-tail is narrow, generally west of the Cascades, from the Columbia River north to the Canadian boundary. Some maps give him a narrow strip running as far south as Baja Peninsula. Hunters have diminished the breed; but hunting season is short, and the birds have their own know-how. Hopefully, they will sur-vive.

The air was filled with drifting seeds, each with its own small parachute—fireweed, dandelion, thistle; a prodigal waste of seeds clung to fir and cedar. Green beans wore fur coats of thistle filaments. Finches of all varieties rode the thistle heads, a great spread feast.

All young had left the nest. The count was made, the year's work accomplished. Adult and juvenile robins flocked. Swallows gathered together and lined the elec-tric wires. Hummingbirds grew fewer in number and ig-nored the syrup in favor of sweet spice pinks, sharing the last of the tritoma with an olive-green warbler. Rumpled streaked young of the rufous-sided towhee scratched for spillings underneath the feeder.

Color along the roadside was largely gold, with occasional aster-purple. Goldenrod showed mustard tones. Golden gumweed lined the shore. Wild yellow mustard came up in clipped meadows and vacant pastures among drifts and crowds of golden-throated oxeye daisies. The sun lacked warmth. This was the year of the green tomato, the immature corn, the maggot in the turnip. Okra, planted hopefully in May, attained a height of six inches.

The first of the army of fall webworms arrived to re- place spring tent caterpillars. Spun silver webs, like gauze bags, enveloped twigs, leaves, and unripened apples, leav- ing storehouses filled with entrapped food for hungry young. Leaves inside turned brown, apples were arrested in mid-growth. Sticky cocoons, like tufts of cotton dipped in syrup, blanketed tree boles, infestations with a timetable.

In the shade of the woods moss glowed red with a queer bloom made up of hundreds of lidded capsules packed with spore. Ripe red huckleberries decorated deli- cate green stems like glass beads on a miniature Christmas tree, each berry a shining bauble filled with juice.

At the head of Oro Bay a single stalk of death camas appeared beside the road. As children in Kansas we called this familiar weed "wild corn." I had never seen it here. One evening I captured a gray and brown moth, with rose- pink stained underwings marked by two blue eyes circled and diagonally banded by black velvet. An eyed hawk moth? It had rested all through the day with eyes folded out of sight under forewings that showed color only at the approach of dusk. Were the eyes apparent to nocturnal creatures?

We dropped the moth into a glass jar and stretched porous muslin across the opening. In the morning the moth lay dead. A cluster of yellowish eggs had been deposited on the cloth. Her life's work stood completed.

The Bat

One evening a long-eared bat hung like a hairy fruit from a leafy twig of the horse chestnut, a strange creature, mammal but not quite animal, winged but not bird, an ugly misfit, shunned but fascinating, comical and yet repulsive. In its long gossamer cloak that flowed from "wrist" to "ankle," it was like an actor employed to emulate a ghoul. Its little eyes looked evil. Its wings were haired instead of feathered.

Imprisoned in a glass jar for the children to watch, it seemed more angry than afraid and went stalking about in circles, its beady eyes glaring. (Bats are near-sighted.) It had an oddly human aspect. Tiny fangs bared, it looked threatening and comically yet chillingly ferocious, evil and pathetic.

I became aware that Hollie, at my side, was crying. "Turn it loose," she whispered. "Let it go."

Off it went into the dusk, strange, unlovely, graceful, symbol of evil, despised and feared without reason. Unable to pigeonhole him into distinct category, steeped in macabre propaganda concerning bats in general, we make of him a vampire, a flying nonbird with forearms, a thing that bears its young alive, that walks and leaves no footprints.

But a bat does leave footprints. In his *Field Guide to Animal Tracks,* mammalogist Olaus Murie shows a sketch of a front wrist and of a hind footprint in sand, the scrape mark of a wing as a Chiroptera takes off in flight. Bats are the only true flying mammals—flying squirrels do not "fly." Some two thousand species inhabit the earth. They hang themselves in rows, head-down, in caves. The sounds they make are frequently too high-pitched for human ears.

How many live here I have no notion. We seemed to have more this past summer, or perhaps I was more often out on foot after dark. Small dark shapes veered and twisted in front of me as I walked. Once I found a brown bat huddled in a cardboard box in the attic. He was like a winged mouse. One hung like a huge hairy moth on the back of a shutter, having crept through a three-quarter-inch crack. During his comparatively long life, a bat is said to consume up to one hundred pounds of insect pests. In flight, he uses his mouth as a trap or employs his cloak as a net. Some bats feed on pollen of night-blooming flowers. Probably no other mammal, save sometimes man, suffers so much undeserved calumny.

Alder by the Brookside

We stood underneath a giant alder loaded with cone clusters, puzzled by a steady pattering as of drops of rain on vanilla leaf and bracken. "Alder seeds!" Jim exclaimed. "Good Lord, no wonder alders come up by the hundreds!"

I have a theory that if all the unsurfaced roads on the Island were to be abandoned and stand unused for a few years they would be discernible from the air by intersecting lines of alder seedlings. Lost in the vicinity of the swamp a few years ago, we found our way out along a grown-over trail by carefully following a phalanx of alder seedlings that all but obliterated a once-cleared entrance.

The trail to the creek follows a kind of shelf cut into the wall of the gulch that terminates at the cove. On the one side grow ferns and ginger, drifts and mats of thimbleberry and vanilla leaf. Near the terminus several hazel bushes have gained a foothold. I had gone down that day to examine these, to see whether jays and chipmunks had left a nut or two. Where the path turns to begin a steeper descent, I stopped in dismay.

Something had happened to the creek, the little brook that runs all year. The stream was no longer there. The entire creek bed as far as I could see was obliterated by heaps of fallen trees. Alder and maple, fir, hemlock, dogwood, and pussy willow lay uprooted, a crazy hodgepodge of fresh, unwithered foliage that bridged the gulch. On the far side, roots torn from the earth had left dens and caves. I could hear the creek but could see no sign of water. A half-uprooted alder lay in the arms of a still-sturdy maple. When a wind blew down the gulch, the alder made a groaning sound.

We had experienced no storm. It was as though a giant hand had been at work. A thought came in the night. Too frequently small private planes disappear over woods, fail, drop through trees and lop off branches, to be buried, finally, in the maelstrom. By morning the thought was more than half conviction. I called a friend and together we searched the area with flashlights, hacking our way through the sea of foliage. We found nothing. Seated on the bank above, we studied the situation and came to the conclusion that the maple had started the cataclysm. Old and weak, its roots softened by the wash of rain, it had given way, striking an alder in its fall. The alder in turn had struck a dogwood, which had struck a second maple. The trees had gone in series, like the dominoes we stood on end in rows as children, tipping the end man to see the others fall.

Vacationing on the Island, Jim and his family set to work with ax, chainsaw, and machete to clear the debris that had buried the old ram and to restore the flow of the creek to its original channel under and through the log dam. Unable to move the big trees that bridged the creek, the workers trimmed away the limbs and left the boles high above the water.

Several months passed before I returned. The change was hardly credible. Ferns and foam flower filled cavities left by torn-out roots. No raw earth showed. Crystal-clear water sang through the hollow log underneath the dam and mirrored colored stones in the stream bed. Best of all were the accidental log bridges. Garmented by fresh growth of yellow-green moss, the spans were crowned with miner's lettuce, mitrewort, violets, tiny red huckleberry, and elder with leaves the size and shape of a mouse's ear. Licorice, sword, and lady fern had struck root. Scattered fronds quivered in air currents created by rapidly moving water.

The tide was at its ebb, the cove empty. Where the waters of the creek diverged to form an alluvial plain of sorts, clumps and hummocks of salt-tolerant grasses formed natural stepping stones above flat mud crisscrossed by tracks, footprints of birds, raccoons, and deer. A cedar stump, marked by an old cut, stood like a sentinel at the entrance to the gulch. A fir tree, rooted in the stump as a seedling, had grown to a height of ninety feet or better. Root branches of the fir, spread like octopus arms to embrace the stump, had embedded in decaying wood. The bleached and barked stump was a totem, a monument engraved with worm hieroglyphics, dotted with holes drilled by woodpeckers, and wearing a fir hairpiece.

In late August the creek moves slowly, with more subdued sound. Rough red berries fallen from madroñas up the gulch rolled with the current. Submerged stones supported masses of attached pupae, imago unknown. Flowing water was filled with look-alike nymphs. How much food for how many lives produced here? How many nymphs would survive to become adult? Was this prodigality a part of a colossal, comprehensive plan?

The tide was far out by the time I had reached the sandspit, the outlet to the cove. Lines of jellyfish with visible viscera, clear blobs without form but with yellowish centers like broken egg yolks, lay stranded. In their element, water, these medusae are graceful and fascinating. On shore they look nondescript and exhausted. Far out, where the waters of the creek divided again to make new

creeks across wet sand, strange objects had come to light
—shoes, bottles encrusted with barnacles, waterlogged
junk. What must the floor of the Sound resemble? Ask any
skindiver. I picked up a log book written in Japanese char-
acters, watersoaked but legible if you could read the language.

A geoduck spurted. Only the knob of his siphon showed,
larger than a silver dollar, his vents wide open. Lately we
have read of tentative requests to harvest these big clams
commercially, by dredge, from deep water. I would be
sorry to see this. I went back up the beach to wait for the
tide to turn. I like to watch the first salt water enter the
cove around the spit, where fresh and salt meet. Flow tide
always seems to come with greater speed. As the water
deepened, a school of elongated fish, like silver needles,
darted up the channel. Algae on the surface made moving
shadows in the sunlit water. In a few moments the geoduck
would be safe until the next low, low tide. Water hurried

up the beach, bringing buoyancy for the jellyfish. Did they still live? Quietly, on a hemlock bough, the kingfisher waited for his incoming supper.

Collomia and Blue Sailors

Along a path that skirts the meadow I found a few scattered blooms of chicory, an escapee (from where? and when?) gone wild. A few come each year despite summer mowing. Blue sailors is another name for this milk-blue tissue flower, a sailor's deserted sweetheart changed by the gods into a flower to stand beside the road and watch and wait. *Cichorium intybus,* no flower that blooms is a truer, gentler blue. The flower lasts but for a day, a delicate ephemeron among luxuriant grasses, a joyous find.

The long taproot, roasted, was and is a substitute for coffee. I have seen only a few of these morning flowers here. During a trip to the slopes of Mount Rainier, in the vicinity of old logging and mining camps, we drove between lines of blue sailors, "found often near the sites of early-day construction camps where it was used during coffee scarcity." The plant grows in abundance on McNeil Island, above Still Harbor, where no doubt it was used as coffee by early loggers or settlers.

I had a taste of chicory-diluted coffee once in New Orleans, a black-as-night brew. "New Orleans coffee," our little hostess told us. "More than half chicory. It's cheaper, but some don't like the dark roast flavor." It seemed appropriate. We had found our way to the place across streets named "Piety," "Patience," and "Plenty."

Collomia was an earlier discovery. Lael and I had set out to walk the three miles from Yoman Point to Higgins Cove—she, at age eight, to flatten beer cans with a vigorous foot and tuck them out of sight in the woods, I, less usefully, to look for plants along the way. But she was the first to see collomia, each flower a terminal cluster of long coral tubes, little trumpet shapes with delicately balanced blue anthers, the color of a baby's eyelids, coral stars with tubular handles. "Tiny trumpets" is a name for another collomia, *linearis,* found in the Rocky Mountains.

We hurried to report the news to Billy Hansen, who marked the plants and gathered seeds. The following spring she brought small specimen plants, which bloomed and seeded and after a few seasons turned escapee. Collomia comes from the word *kolla,* meaning "glue." Drop a seed of collomia into water and a sticky mucus forms and diffuses to surround the seed with a smoke-like cloud.

Each animal, each plant, seeks its own favorite habitat. Underneath a bower of tall firs one mild August afternoon, I came suddenly upon a drift of rattlesnake plantain, a rare greenish-white orchid with rosettes of striped and latticed leaves, growing in a spongy accumulation of brown needle drop. The flowers grow in loose spirals, the upper sepals united with the petals to form a helmet known as a galea. Not every summer produces bloom. I had seen the plant, but not in flower and only at an altitude of ten thousand feet, on Cucharas Pass in the Colorado Rockies. Guidebooks distinguish rattlesnake plantain as "a plant of high altitudes." How had it come at sea level on a saltwater island? The name results from an Indian belief that some portions of the plant provided a specific for snakebite. According to Erna Gunther, the Cowlitz Indians of the Northwest make it into a tea which is used as a tonic. She also learned from a Klallam informant that women formerly rubbed the plant on their bodies to make their husbands like them better.

Thistles

*"Must be purple is a weed
And pink and white is posies."*

(EDNA ST. VINCENT MILLAY)

Our various thistles are late bloomers. Names are descriptive—bristle and bull, elk and milk, bur and woolly, creeping and cursed. They run in waves, an armed scourge, beautiful and belligerent, with silver-lined leaves, hoary heads, and sometimes a delightful fragrance.

Great and small, they bloomed in late July and throughout August in shades of purple, rose, and lavender. One species with small numerous heads of rose-magenta gave off a heady sweetness for yards around, an unapproachable, despised plant possessed of invisible virtue. We are too quick to judge. In Yellowstone Park in 1870 a very near-sighted man named Truman Everts strayed from his party and broke his glasses, a nightmare of all spectacle-wearers. Unable to find his way, desperate and near starvation, Everts uprooted a thistle, *Cirsium foliosum*. History does not say why he chose this particular species, only that he ate the root and was refreshed and strengthened. For a month he lived on thistle root. Eventually he was rescued. The common name of *foliosum*, right enough, is "Everts' thistle."

Please take note, all wanderers: Any and all thistles are said to be safe and would sustain man in such emergency. Almost any thistle is spectacular, strongly or weakly armed, *lanceolatum* to *edule*. They grow in masses, bristled camps topped with color like flying flags. Their seeds are a favorite food of finches.

September

After Labor Day

By the first of September green-spined balls had grown to golf-ball size among palmlike foliage of the horse chestnut tree, cases that would burst in another month to eject shining seeds, both beautiful and bitter. Horse chestnut is not a buckeye, but both are of the buckeye family, genus *Aesculus*. Nuts of both have eyes and are said to bring good luck.

During the unlucky thirties a sad-eyed huckster stood on a downtown street in Kansas City offering "lucky buckeyes" for a quarter. "If I had two bits," a bystander remarked dryly, "I could make my own luck." Some must have faith. In a news bulletin published weekly in Atlanta, Georgia, "lucky buckeyes" are advertised each autumn. For all their bad taste, I have a theory that the deer eat these. We find trampled pods, the seeds cleared away, and deer tracks abundant underneath the trees.

Vine maples with leaves of translucent scarlet were the high mark of September. More shrub than tree, vine maple chooses its own background, spreading brilliant leaves to form a studied mosaic against somber green of conifer or gray dappled bole of alder. They steal the spotlight, demand attention, cry out with color. Each leaf is like a dancer in a scarlet tutu. The Otso Point Road between the Johnson farm and schoolhouse hill is a trail of splendor that dips and rises. Low spots are seeps, even in dry weather. The swamp is just out of sight, behind tall trees hung with long gray beards of lichen.

By September crowns of broadleaf maple had commenced to yellow and to shed the first plate-sized leaves. During all of our years here, the road had been given scant attention. No clearing had been done, and no building marred its length. Two vehicles would have been hard-pressed to find a passing width. Traces of log crossings laid by pioneers remained. Only an occasional dim trail made by woodcutters or by deer entered the woods on either side. A patch of twisted stalk, a kink-stemmed lily called "white mandarin" or "liverberry," bloomed in one spot each spring, hung single tiny cream bells from bases of parallel-veined, clasping leaves. Even the thin wire stems that supported the flowers were kinked. The ovary of each flower became by fall an egg-shaped bright red berry.

Suddenly the road was opened, widened, tiled, and

graded. Plastic flags and surveyors' stakes appeared. Trimming admitted unaccustomed light, and shade-loving growth receded. Seeps dried away. Cycle riders found the dips a challenge. But after Labor Day most of these were gone. Shallow swales were once again hushed places. Bright red samara of vine maple that had escaped the trimming-back stood at right angles to scarlet twigs, like the wings of brilliant butterflies. Even on gray days, the bright, clear leaves gave an illusion of sunlight.

Wild cucumbers ripened, egg-sized burs filled with brown seeds reminiscent of the round button fruits of Kentucky coffee we used as children in the game of jackstones.

Our Canadian cousin discovered the abandoned nest of a rufous hummingbird on the low limb of a pear tree directly above the path we had all traveled a hundred times. As wide across as a silver dollar, the tiny cup was coated with flecks of gray-green lichen, camouflaged to resemble the scores of lichen-encrusted joints and knobs and scars on limbs and twigs throughout the crown. In-curved at the margin, lined with dandelion and thistle floss and bits of moss and lichen, the nest looked too small to have accommodated even a rufous family.

One rainy morning we found that the ripe corn patch had been invaded. Not a single ear remained. Cobs lay in the mud, stripped clean of every kernel. I scanned the eleven-foot fence surrounding the garden, topped by strands of barbed wire. How could a raccoon negotiate that fence? No single raccoon, or three or four, gluttons though they are, could clean a corn patch in a night. I found a hole a foot off the ground, the size of a basketball, wires clipped neatly as though by scissors.

In pastures and uncut meadows, moving seas of oxeye daisies gave place to Queen Anne's lace, forerunner of the garden carrot, a plant with finely dissected leaves and foamy umbels of small white flowers in which a purple flower or two are frequently embedded. After the petals drop, the flower heads form a cup, giving rise to a second common name of bird's nest fern.

Car headlights shone on a cottontail rabbit fleeing for his life, an owl in pursuit. The night was pitch black. No sound broke the silence, no rabbit scream of pain and terror. The rabbit had escaped. What kind of owl? Kitchin recorded four owls as year-around Island residents—Kennicott's screech, dusky horned, coast pygmy, saw-whet. He named a fifth—the short-eared, *Asio flammeus*—as winter visitor. The voice of the screech owl brings shivers.

I have not seen the horned owl, but I hear his voice sometimes, a rhythmic, resonant call, a sweet strange music, like African drums. The voice of an owl is deceptive as to distance and direction. I walked up the road from the ferry slip one night with the evening paper and heard a screech owl call from McNeil Island. Or so I thought. But an owl is a ventriloquist. The deception adds to his power over those in whom his voice strikes terror—the warbler on her nest, the vole, the rabbit in his burrow.

Most pleasant voices were stilled by the first of September. Cowbirds grated among the shrubbery. Underneath the holly boughs, yellowing now with berries, a rufous-sided towhee sounded the same monotonous note over and over. A slim California creeper probed the bark of the red-berried cotoneaster with his thin curved bill, nipped across to the base of the Spitzenberg apple, and began a spiral ascent, his stiff tail braced, working as he climbed.

I watched a mother robin in the birdbath attempt to teach a youngster from her second brood by splashing water in his face. But he would have none of learning. He teetered on the edge, interested only in the knot of angleworms she held as though she offered a bribe. She flew away with the bribe, ignoring his protest. No bath, no food. He set off in hot pursuit and was replaced by a hermit thrush that dropped like a brown leaf.

Autumn Equinox

A wind whipped up rolling waves that carried logs across the road and left them stranded. Sand was salt-and-pepper color, "shell sand" in ridges and terraces, made up of bits of shells, ground by stones in a hammer mill of water. The sand was filled with young life, moving snails barely attached to tiny thread-screw shells, baby ghost shrimps, joint worms, coral colored delicate pink clams no larger than half a fingernail, snow-white skeletons of sand dollars the size of buttons on a baby dress and exquisitely patterned.

I sat down to watch the killdeers feed. In constant motion, they left a crazy stitch of tracks. Their cries sounded lonely, but they were a family. Thimbleberry along the bank was defoliated by deer. Bracken had turned a purple-bronze color, but still looked crisp and neat. Air was heavy near the orchard with the smell of ripening apples. I could hear them drop. Reverse sides of sword fern fronds were intricately embroidered with bright orange spore cases on every pinnule. The last traces of trillium—blossom, leaf, and stem—were gone until another spring. A few remaining three-lobed flowers, the color of dried blood, hid underneath mats of heart-shaped wild ginger leaves. The runners gave off a spicy smell. Petals of the bell-shaped corollas have long, curious, trailing tails.

In marshy fields, true rushes wore tufts of bloom. Long, armed briars of Himalaya climbed the weathered boards of Peterson's unfinished barn, begun years before the builder's death and destined never to be completed, probably, a monument plastered with No Trespassing signs. The Peterson house was reduced to ashes on a cold New Year's

Day. A narrow gate with birdhouse on a post still gives access and a few scattered boards form a sidewalk that goes nowhere. Curio seekers stop along the road and go inside to pick among the shards of broken glass and twisted metal, grown over now with sedge and nettle.

By September, rose bushes beyond the spray area were hung with bright hips, a fruit, rich in vitamin C, that has saved lives. The little shrub called snowberry or waxberry bore thick clusters of oddly shaped, waxy-white berries. Untouched (so far as I know) by bird or animal, these stay on all winter.

The Swamp

Accompanied by a friend, one September afternoon, I made an expedition in to the swamp, which occupies several acres below the Ekenstam-Johnson Road in mid-Island. I had visited the lower end of the swamp many times, going in along a trail made by Lowell Johnson for the removal of firewood or of garden peat, the black spongy residue left when the water evaporated away during a dry summer. Prior to that day I had not entered from the upper side, and never in September, when growth is at a standstill and the air is permeated with a smell of ripening and the fine flying dust from hundreds of varieties of pollen.

From Otso Point Road, a path used by deer and woodcutters ran in a little way and abruptly ended, with no indication that either man or animal had penetrated further. Looped bluish canes of thorny blackcap, thimbleberry, wild gooseberry and salmonberry, and stinging nettle, lover of marshy, semishaded earth, had created a jungle through which we literally fought our way, led by an eerie kind of light that meant space without trees.

The marsh has no distinct shore line, even in wet weather. During dry weather it is a vignette with frayed growth edges. Because of the dry spell just passed, the water had receded to the size of a small pond, green and stagnant, crowded with life, a shrunken, overpopulated world, swarming with mosquitoes. Horned water striders skated in and out among exhausted-looking lily pads, and a drift of cat-tails with brown, cigar-shaped heads on long unbranched stems grew in and out of the water. Each head was topped by a short defoliated stem from which pollen had shattered, a small antenna.

Yellow cup-shaped pond lilies with knobbed centers stood up on fleshy spikes anchored in dried mud. The plant is also known as cowlily and spatterdock. Indians called it wokas and roasted and ate the seeds, which are said to taste like popcorn. In hard times they consumed the large, scaly, tangled rootstocks. We watched a blue dragonfly with double pairs of thin gauze wings dance in and out among the cat-tails and come to rest on a little dwarf sedge, a bur reed with tiny armed fruits and triangular keeled leaves. Unexplained bubbles winked like silver eyes in the green water, and we spotted an emerald frog that sat motionless beneath crossed blades of wild rush. On the bare dead limb of a drowned dogwood tree a red-tailed hawk

held silent vigil. At midafternoon with a wan sun shining, the place had a sleepy look. Here was a world not ours; amphibian and strange, it belonged to those that made it home. We spoke of being glad that no road led in.

When we turned to go, we discovered that we had lost all sense of direction. It was as though the brambles through which we had beaten our way had closed in behind us. If deer came here to drink, they left no path. Beyond a thicket of alder seedlings, we came into conifer woods where big rough-barked firs presented overlapping shelves of giant fungi with lilac or pale green undersurfaces. We tried to break off one of these, but it was so firmly embedded in the tissue of the tree that it bore our weight. Concentric bands of orange, gray, and shades of brown lined the caps of these big woody polypores, which seemed to mark off yet another world where we were interlopers. Still without a notion as to north or east or west or south, we chose a deer path that brought us out a full quarter of a mile from the point of entry where we had left our car, and around a corner.

Indian Summer

With the roads bare of traffic, deer became much bolder. We went on deer counts of evenings, slow drives over the network of Island roads. To see twenty or more in a half hour's time was not uncommon. Five or six deer in dark fall coats appeared each evening on the meadow and worked their way down as the night deepened. In the mornings the earth was clean of windfall apples.

We stood outside one night at nine and watched a doe pick and choose in the back yard. A deer never seems to eat; it merely tastes. She took half a fig leaf, a grape shoot, a twig of mock orange, a Tropicana rosebud. If we made a move she turned to face us, her ears like signal flags. Her eyes shone red-gold in the light from the kitchen window. Her steps made no sound at all.

Lael asked, "May we speak now?" "All right," I said. We heard the quiver of boards in the rail fence, the rustle of overhanging pear boughs, and nothing further.

Chipmunks increased their activity, chattered in the trees, took holly berries and seeds from windfall apples, appeared and disappeared. If we tried to follow, they led us on wild-goose chases, zigged and zagged, stood on hind legs and looked back over their shoulders, scolding our advances.

Opportunist convolvulus with pink-ribbed, funnel-shaped corollas opened along a new fill. Wide awake of mornings and wet with dew, they closed of afternoons. White musk-mallow bloomed, a stranger, not native, a little hollyhock. Stamens form a tube around the pistil. Cones carpeted the earth underneath the firs, a good cone year. Foresters say such years run in cycles. The chipmunk gathered seeds and dashed back and forth across the road, as though he anticipated a hard winter.

Shrinking Indian summer days were filled with a new and warmer light. Red-shafted flickers chattered in the trees and took off from the road, calling "wicky, wicky, wicky" and flashing white rump patches. Wings and tail of these chisel-billed *Picidae* with zygodactyl feet are lined with salmon color. Cheerfully noisy birds with black front bibs and polka-dotted vests, they seem mavericks in the woodpecker family; they pull worms from the earth and associate with robins. Even jays back down sometimes before the rapier beak of the red-moustached male.

Days remained mild and hazy, but nights turned chilly. Baneberry, which had bloomed inconspicuously in May, set handsome scarlet fruits in moist shaded places. In the lee of high shore banks, young gulls gathered in flocks and held noisy convocations. They looked brand new, clean and innocent, and moved all at once, like leaves before a puff of wind. Alder and broadleaf maple turned a slow yellow. In Leta Thornton's primary room in Liberty, Kansas, we drew around maple leaves and made colored cutouts to paste on autumn windows. I would like to hear the "oh's" and "ah's" if I had taken one of these, as big as chair cushions.

Edible and Inedible Fungi

Rain fell in the night, and the mercury dropped in the thermometer. On lawns and open meadows, *Agaricus campestris*, white-capped mushrooms with pale pink gills that turned dark in a day, appeared in abundance. They come so quickly you can watch the veil rupture and the cap open like an unfurled umbrella. The more vigorous specimens emerged in the pasture, from dung heaps dropped by cattle. Once mature, they become worm-infested, with slug-nibbled edges.

In Kansas pastures we gathered these edible meadow mushrooms in both spring and fall seasons. Here they appear only in the autumn, "when temperatures drop to 59 degrees," according to our mushroom mentor, Sam Tokarczyk of the ferry *Islander*. Even more abundant are clusters of small round or pear-shaped puffballs that spring up like clutches of eggs among them. Taken young and tender with centers still snow-white, puffballs serve as *Agaricus* extenders.

Overnight, all manner of fungi put in an appearance in both shade and sun, in intriguing shapes and flower colors. Boletes with maroon caps and yellow pores competed with rosy *Russula* and purple *Cortinarius*. In open woods, brown needle carpets were dotted with upstanding yellow and cream-coral *Clavaria cristata*. Once, in deeper woods, I came across a patch of yolk-yellow chantarelle, lily-shaped and with a delicate smell of ripe apricots. Off-white oyster mushrooms (*Pleurotus ostreatus*) like frail shells grew in tight clusters on decaying stumps and logs and sometimes on living trees.

In a small cleared area on the shore of Lake Josephine, a dozen varieties decorated the clipped grass. Lead-gray inky

caps like little South Sea island huts turned to black fluid in your hand. Admirable boletus grew side by side with smoky elfin saddles and big brown helvellas that had an evil guise. New frontage roads, scraped clean of green vegetation, were carpeted with bright orange "fairy cups" (*Aleuria aurantia*), tender and with a buttery flavor. Pale yellow, sticky jelly fungi, shaped like human ears, covered rotting wood. Along shaded Guthrie Road, warty-capped amanitas in orange, yellow, and red—the most beautiful and most deadly of all—emerged among brown fallen leaves. It is said that amanitas account for over 90 percent of the deaths from mushroom poisoning and that the poison takes effect quickly. The name of "fly amanita" came of a belief that a witches' brew made from this particular species is lethal to the common fly. Unable to resist their beauty, I carried them home and set them in flower pots in rows, a witch's garden. Each day I brought home fresh and different specimens, made delicate spore prints, and thumbed through guides and slides in an effort at identification. The entire house smelled of mushrooms, a pleasant, earthy odor, but I did not learn much.

October

The Duck That Went to Prison

Birds that make their homes along a waterfront accept with equanimity the coming and going of whatever boats. Dock-side gulls, sometimes injured or crippled, readily make friends with unemployed men who hang about waterfronts to watch boats come and go, with passengers who wait, with fishermen and children, and with the rootless who have nowhere else to go. I have watched men who looked out-of-pocket buy popcorn or peanuts from concessions to feed a hungry shore bird or wild fowl.

191

One day last summer, the Ehrickes' eleven-year-old daughter Nancy found a young wild duckling in the busy driveway that gives access to her father's machine shop and garage. Where the duck came from we never knew. It simply materialized, a hungry ball of fuzz no bigger than the egg it came from. Someone remembered having heard of a duckling surviving a drop by hawk or crow in flight, but no one quite believed the theory.

The duckling became a household (indeed, an Island) pet, a one-duck public zoo. In the manner of a solitary domestic duck, she followed members of the family and made friends with all who came. Having discovered the beach, she crossed the road several times a day to mine mud and gravel and ricks of seaweed. Passing Islanders learned to watch out for Duck. Nancy painted the word L⊕VE in big chartreuse letters across the county roadway to serve as a crosswalk.

I was sorry not to be on hand the day Duck discovered flight. She had grown a good deal by then, and wing feathers had sprouted. Down had been replaced by a fine-speckled brownish coat with a wing bar of soft blue. Some inner voice said "fly," and she was airborne. Nancy's mother Sylvia watched. Just watching must have been akin to flying. Duck sailed across the lawn, over the road, down the beach, and literally belly-flopped into the water.

After that there was no keeping her. Nancy decided, with wisdom beyond her years, that Duck should not be wing-clipped. "I want her to mate and raise babies." Flights lengthened. Nancy left for school on an early morning ferry, and Duck was lonely. As though she wondered about this huge waddling thing that walked on water, Duck flew down to the ferry slip, to sit on the bridge or crossbar. One day as the ferry was about to sail, she went aboard. She disembarked at Steilacoom and spent the day on the dock accepting handouts from delighted docksiders. She came home to roost in her protected pen for a time, but seafaring was in her blood. She became a regular on the ferry, a pampered passenger. No one knew why she chose to land one day at the federal penitentiary, to make her way up the road to the prison compound. We heard that she took her meals in the dining room and that she was everybody's pet. We had news of her from commuting guards. She lived high on the prison menu. But one day the news was distressing. A helpless tower guard, at his post on the wall of the compound, saw a raccoon (likewise a pet) pounce on Duck, the trusting, and carry her away.

At the opposite pole are feral cats that manage to survive the perils of unwanted and uncared-for kittenhood. I see them along the road or in the woods, cats as wild as cougars and far more cautious than deer. They take a heavy toll of birds and rodents, as do domestic cats, but they strike a sympathetic chord. Generations removed from domesticity, they lead strange lives. They breed, but only the toughest and the fittest survive. I find dead kittens about abandoned buildings, starved, deserted by the mother cat and unable to fend for themselves, or killed by malevolent toms, a pathetic lot. If all survived, birds and chipmunks would suffer irretrievable losses. I should become case-hardened, but never do.

One that *did* survive, a tough little rough-coated tom with bunchy side whiskers and remarkably long hair (fancy blood back there somewhere), lives in the big unused barn at the end of our road. Wilder than any raccoon, he is sometimes forced by hunger to approach the house, especially during the winter when his game is scarce. A beautiful cat, with golden eyes, he positions himself well back from the door to wait in mute appeal for a handout. I have never heard him make a sound. I may not have seen him for a month or more, and then I come out one morning to start the coffee and there he sits, as inscrutable as a stone cat, his eyes beamed on the pantry window.

I hurry with his food. He is especially fond of warm

milk, and he looks half-starved. I try to make friends but he will have none of my importunities. I open the door to set the dishes outside and call softly but he runs, to crouch behind the heather, and declines to move a step until I am back inside with the door closed. He approaches cautiously, keeping close to earth and looking up at the window and back over his shoulders. He eats ravenously but uneasily, stopping periodically to study my face at the window. He may come each morning for a while. He fills out. His gray-gold coat smoothes and brightens. Incongruously, his favorite foods are "civilized," gravies and sauces.

Save that he is more handsome, he bears a strong resemblance to our lazy neutered house cats and so we have named him Big Daddy, though he is far smaller than they. I would like to make friends, to let him know somehow that I respect and admire his wildness and his spirit. But he is not to be won over. A few times I have taken his dish to his heather fortress, tried to woo him with soothing talk. If he is sufficiently hungry, he stands his ground but spits a warning, and I retreat.

Even our domestic cats elicit his contempt. He tolerates their curious investigations of his person but makes no response. As soon as he has finished eating, he departs with grace and dignity. He despises all things human or domestic. His acceptance of our welfare is solely for survival. He would like us to know that, if he could make it on his own, he would have none of our largess or charity.

Time of Asters

After the rains and winds of the autumn equinox, the weather softened again and the skies cleared. Feathered migrants lingered as though reluctant to start the long flights and chipmunks renewed their harvest. Roadsides, washed by rains, gleamed with ripe huckleberries. The leaves looked polished. Flat red insipid fruits decorated maple-leafed thimbleberry, and salal and mahonia concealed waxy clusters of blackish-purple berries that would remain on half the winter. Blue elderberry was *indigo*. Ripe grass stems bent with the weight of goldfinches.

Purple and gold are October colors. Goldenrod spires darkened to the color of Chinese mustard. Influenced by salt spray, flowers of gumweed remained bright gold, and yellow and orange calendulas and marigolds in the garden took on new impetus. Best of all the wildflowers and most persistent were wide-awake asters and purple fleabane with golden eyes, the flowers shading from palest lavender to deepest violet. The "eyes" are little disk flowers. I call them all Michaelmas because I like the name, which refers to the festival of the Archangel Michael, celebrated on September 29 in Britain. "Christmas daisies" is another name for these hardy and late-blooming flowers. On hazy October afternoons they have a sleepy look. Even trained botanists hesitate to edge out on the limb of distinguishing species.

From a wine-tipped dogwood tree in second flower, one October morning, there came a whistled, lonely-sounding note, repeated over and over. With the aid of glasses, I was able, finally, to locate the piper, a slim gray bird with white eye ring, almost robin size but more erect and streamlined. With the further help of guidebook and recording, I identified him as Townsend's solitaire. A loner, the solitaire is out of place here, a transient from a higher altitude. Had our ripe fruits brought him down, perhaps? He has a song that I would like to hear, a sweet, prolonged warble, but he favored us only with this single plaintive note.

Clear leaves of cottonwood drifted earthward. Each leaf spiraled slowly, turning and twisting in air as though to scout a suitable landing site. Unlike the leathery leaves of madroña, they fall in silence. Each morning the earth car-

pet boasted a new layer of fresh gold. Leaves of broadleaf
maple seemed to come down all at once, like loads of earth
from a dump truck. In margins of green conifer woods,
patches of gold surrounded the trees and reflected light
upward, as though each skeleton stood on stage, spotlighted
from a projection room.

A Safe Place

On an evening of cloud drift and leaf fall I overtook a
very small girl who walked along an Island road. Her coat
hung open and her head was bare. Her arms were filled
with purple Michaelmas. When she turned, her small face
wore a serene and happy look. The thought occurred that
she was a long way from any house for so late an hour
and for so small a girl; but she declined politely my offer
of a ride. "I'm just out for a *walk*," she said. "My walk's
not finished yet."

As though she were afraid that I might insist or that my
feelings might be hurt by her refusal, she added, "I'm going
down the road to see a *friend. She's* been sick and I'm taking her some flowers." She held the flowers up for me to
see. I nodded and drove on, watching through the rear-
vision mirror. She did, indeed, turn into a driveway after
a while, a road that led to a house far back, on a hill. May
the time never come when a child will be unsafe alone on
these tree-lined roads. A child needs to be alone in the
country, to feel secure. Nothing lives on this Island that
would harm a youngster. Save occasionally, on summer
week ends since the improvement of certain roads by
asphalt, traffic presents no danger. Except at such times,
parents have no need to warn their children against accepting rides with strangers. In a community so small and
so circumscribed, there *are* no strangers.

Whither Come, Whither Go?

One day out of three the sun crept up the sky to shine like a blessing for an hour. But clouds came soon after and drizzle began. When the wind blew in from the east, you could taste salt in the falling rain. When the wind blew hard, salt spray drenched the windows. Air was damp and chilly, but not cold. Apple trees, deceived by springlike weather, burst into a second blooming and even set fruit. Sporadic flowers peered out from among the long hairy pods of Scotch broom, which burst with a soft explosive sound.

After the last of the swallows had gone, the air over the meadow seemed empty. Straggling flocks of crows flew over. In one flock a solitary member was set upon and pecked time after time by various members of the assembly. At last he dropped away, to sit lonely and disconsolate in a tree. What sin had he committed, to be shunned by his fellows? Where would he go now? A second group came over, but he made no effort to join them.

White-crowned sparrows were gone, too. They had slipped quietly away, along with the last of the humming-birds and the summer robins. New swimmers appeared off-shore, long-necked grebes, surf scoters blown in from the ocean, diving ducks with brilliant patches that blazed like orange flames in the sun. They did not dive all at once, but went down in a one–two–three–four pattern, at seemingly timed intervals, from a parade line and surfaced the same way, bobbing up without a splash. You could have set it all to music.

One morning the feeder and the ivy below swarmed with juncos that must have come in the night, from mountain nesting grounds. Towhees scratched and scrabbled on the board, and juncos ate the spillings. Two Steller's jays settled on the porch outside the window, dislodging and swallowing flecks of floor enamel. Would they die of lead poisoning? When I knocked on the window, they leapt away. One junco had lost a foot, leaving a leg like a bit of broken toothpick. He slanted in and landed on the one remaining foot, using his tail for balance.

Some days the sun favored us with an evening encore. Then, sunsets were spectacular, gray sky enriched with muted shades of rose and apricot and orange. The ragged Olympic Range was blue-white in silhouette, and snow line crept lower on the peaks. Hours of daylight shortened. As the ferry approached the dock of mornings, we heard the wail of the guiding siren. On windless evenings the smell of coumarin came up strong from browning vanilla leaf. Old orchards were bright with reddening apples, and woods glowed with yellowed alder.

One night I heard the musical whicker of a horned owl, a haunting sound in broken rhythm, repeated at minute intervals. Night after night I returned to the same spot, hoping to hear the call again or to catch a glimpse of the caller. An enormous bird, with close to five-foot wing span, the great horned has an appetite to match his size. His "horns" are not *horns,* but ear tufts.

Once more the salamanders were out in migration, but now most of them moved in the opposite direction, away from breeding grounds. We saw them by the hundreds, a relentless procession into wet woods, and we found hundreds of them dead in the roads, crushed beyond recognition. How many more must have survived before the encroachment of civilization!

During all of September a seagull spent his days and possibly his nights on a neighbor's round cushion-shaped float. One day in late October he was replaced by a cormorant, and the gull came only occasionally when the cormorant was away. I missed the contest if there was one. The cormorant stood for long periods with his wings spread-eagled. He appeared to face the wind deliberately. His wings blew back; his bill was pointed skyward like the beak of a bittern. With his wings folded, or in flight, he is a snaky, homely bird, but with his wings outspread, he has a majestic look.

A male rufous hummingbird appeared and danced on whirring wings about the few remaining fuchsia blossoms. He investigated the late-blooming snapdragons and swept up and over the roof to touch the first flowers of *Prunus autumnalis.* We hurried to get the feeder out, but he was gone. He never came again.

A rumor persisted that a mother bear and two cubs had been seen on Larson Road. One day along this road I encountered a big bushy raccoon that had somehow lost his tail. He stood on hind legs and watched my approach. In half dusk, at four in the afternoon, he somewhat resembled a bear until he dropped to all fours and humped into the underbrush. As I turned off the main road onto a fern-choked trail, I found myself trying to recall advice or counsel heard or read about bear encounters. Did one shout, or speak softly, or pretend to be a post and make no sound or movement at all? I have not climbed a tree since childhood. Even the lowest limbs of the tall naked alders looked a long way up and too frail to bear my weight. When a fir bough, blown loose from somewhere landed with a soft "plop" in the path and the air was filled suddenly with a rustling flurry of yellow maple leaves, I increased my speed.

More than rumor is the word that coyotes have been seen and heard. One evening we saw a coyote on the shore of East Oro Bay. A beautiful and playful-seeming animal, he gave no evidence of fear, although he must have seen us. He appeared preoccupied with leaping down the high bank to the beach and climbing up again, to lope gracefully about in circles. Since then others have heard the evening serenade, and thought there were two coyotes or more. One coyote can sound like half a dozen. I remember Kansas coyotes that answered the nightly whistle of the ten-forty train as it approached the local crossing, a staccato barking, with musical overtones.

November

Hunters

As deer season approached, Islanders nailed up an unprecedented number of No Hunting signs. All during the spring and summer we had complained of deer damage in yards and gardens, but now we were on the side of the deer. We felt protective, and looked forward with dread and a certain resentment to the invasion of red-hatted strangers in trucks and campers, on motorcycles and on foot, antici-

pating deer taken to be a personal as well as a community
loss.

A few hunters came early, before the season opened, and
shot deer in the roads of nights, using spotlights to blind
the animals. These did the deer a service I suppose; for with
the first shots fired the hunted vanished into deep woods.
Hunters complained bitterly of "posted" signs and accused
Islanders of having "killed off all the bucks." I am always
personally intrigued during hunting season by the bucks'
especial savvy. How does a buck know that he is marked
for the killing? The does seem less afraid. Some hunters
looked too young to carry the big guns, and these were the
most eager, the least apt to respect restrictions. We saw
pretty, armed girls, in scarlet outfits, and wondered whether
they had read *Bambi*.

From daylight until long after dusk, we heard the sound
of guns in old and broken orchards. Occasionally a dead
doe was found abandoned, because of the penalty for killing
does. We stayed out of the woods, feeling in small part the
fear I suppose the deer must know, and looked forward to
the end of open season. Bow-and-arrow time saw a few
Robin Hoods in picturesque garb. But an arrow, too, in the
hands of the careless can make a nasty wound and not kill.

Bucks that had stood tall enough to harvest plums and
apples left the Island tied to radiators and trunks of cars,
feet shackled together, lovely lifeless heads hanging. I have
no taste for venison. One young hunter who looked under-
age could hardly contain his pride. Waiting for the ferry to
carry him back to the mainland, he strutted and boasted,
patted the carcass as lovingly and fondly as a mother would
caress her child. He recounted the adventure with young
eyes shining, relived the chase, the shot, the wounding, the
animal's attempt at escape, the final denouement, "straight
between the eyes. Dropped like he'd been poleaxed. I let
him have another one for good measure. Sometimes they
get up. Then look out!"

The boy's shirt sleeves were rolled to the elbows, garments, hands, arms dark with dried blood. He unwrapped and ate a sandwich as he talked and gestured.

The buck with the big rack no longer came to the Wealthy tree outside the pantry window. Throughout September and October he had appeared on the meadow at dusk, working his way gradually toward house and orchard. We heard and saw him sometimes of nights. He made a snuffling sound as he searched through ivy ground cover for fallen apples. On moonlit nights his rack of horns when he raised his head resembled tree branches.

One morning when I went to the pantry to start breakfast he was still there. Had the window been open I could have touched him. Our eyes met. His expression after a moment was one of gentleness and trust. Or so I thought. He went back to munching apple. I have no doubt that his rack was his undoing. His head would have made a spectacular trophy. We heard he was gutshot, went down twice, but arose each time, and finally escaped into the trees. A trail of blood led through the wood, across a second meadow, over an open road into a second wood, and was lost in a gulch. The hunter searched throughout the day but never found his game.

"Either sex" season brought fresh scores of hunters. A pickup truck cruised the roads with guns bristling in all directions, nimrods seated comfortably on chairs in the back. Hunters sprawled on trunks and hoods. One young girl had brought a saddle-shaped stool for waiting comfort. We saw her several times beside a road that led to an old orchard.

But eventually all seasons ended, and we went back to normal. I resumed my walks but saw few deer. The animals would remain shy until well into the new year. Some days now the skies were black with ducks. In times of storm, wildfowl in migration filled the coves and inlets, and we heard the sound of guns again. Duck season would continue into January. Personally, I disliked this killing, too. But these were migrants or casual visitors and did not seem (as do the deer) members of our Island family.

Along Came a Spider

The air held a hint of frost and smelled of autumn. Bright red honeysuckle berries decorated defoliating shrubs, and madroña boles darkened to mahogany color. Water roughened and gleamed with whitecaps. Boats quartered into the waves. Red-brown spiders with long legs and queer knobbed pincers, like the antennae of butterflies, moved inside the house. Each morning a spider or two appeared in the bathtub, to be carried outside again. The following morning an identical spider was in the tub.

Thirty thousand species of spiders have been named, and this is believed to be only about one-fourth the total. A spider is not an insect, but an arachnid, as are mites and scorpions. Most spiders have eight simple eyes. They have four pairs of legs. The two subdivisions of the body, cephalothorax and abdomen, distinguish Arachnida from Insecta.

From spinnerets on the spider's abdomen come silken threads produced as a fluid pressed out of spinning tubes. On contact with air, the liquid thread solidifies and becomes a cable composed of many individual threads. Some spiders build egg cocoons or sperm webs, others line burrows or make trap doors with hinges. Webs may be domes, bowls, funnels, tubes, triangles, or geometric orbs with a central hub and many radii. A spider may construct his own tent, or he may hide in a leaf and hold a guy line connected to the center of his web. As with a fisherman, vibration of the line tells him when he has a captive.

The young spiderling (or spiderlet) leaves the nest on a thread of his own silk, launched forth as on a flying trapeze, using the thread as a kind of parachute to ride the air. I find these in the washbowl, no larger than a good-sized pinhead. A slowly circling finger at a distance of several inches will pick up an invisible thread by means of which I can carry the spiderlet outside. Spiderlings have been found floating on these threads five miles high. Brought down by a whim of air current, the little traveler sets to work to become an adult, to spin a home, a trap for food. Wild oats sown, he settles down to fulfill his purpose, to eat and procreate. *He* may be eaten by *her* after mating.

"No fear of the future . . . "

Cold rain fell. Band-tailed pigeons gathered in the madroña trees. One bird stood watch while the others fed on the rough red berries. At a signal, trees exploded blue-gray pigeons that were gone in seconds, plunging into fir boughs that closed to receive them. Pigeons, too, have their time of being hunted.

A downy woodpecker made his orderly way around the laurel tree. Seen close up, with his white vest and rows of white wing buttons, he had a clean furred look. All of the trees in the yard are decorated by his artistry.

With defoliation came new vistas in the woods, that third dimension. Last summer's hidden nests came to light, and the forest took on fresh perspective. The air was redolent with an evocation of pitch and leafmold and a smell of mushrooms. I touched a crumbling stump with my boot toe and it disintegrated into odd geometric shapes, tunneled by worms and beetles into a labyrinth of intercommunication. With one touch I had destroyed an entire city. Death had no finality here for life fed on death.

Sunlight sketched moving shadows on gray boles of alders and highlighted the rich bronze-red of prickly Oregon grape. Poison oak was red, too. All along the neck of Oro Bay, this shrub, which is not oak but sumac, cast scarlet reflections in the water. "Leaves three, leave it be!" we learned as children. But sometimes poison oak has five.

In November each tree stands out as an individual even in a forest. Trees, when you come to know them, no more

resemble one another than do men in a crowd of men. Some accident or condition of environment, some prevailing wind has bent and shaped and influenced the seedling. Wounds heal and leave scars. Old trees like old men and women bear cicatrices of past abrasions. Limbs reach for light wherever light is available, bend and twist, and grope upward and outward. Roots grow deep in dry seasons. Some years are good, some bad, and bands of tissue widen and narrow in response. Trees that survived a bad beginning may stand more staunchly and live for a longer time.

Children who grow up on the plains form attachments for individual trees. A man transplanted from the Southwest remembers certain trees as "first base" and "second base." For my sister Elsie and me, special trees, widely scattered, were the homes of imaginary friends, stations on the maps of our minds. *The* "thornberry." *The* hackberry. *The* "coffee bean" (Kentucky coffee). Certain persimmons bore the sweetest fruit. We *knew*. I can still see in memory individual sycamores, the plane trees with glistening heart-shaped leaves. Bark came off in sheets and left a tender green-cream color. These trees were our companions. In his 1869 journal, undertaken during a sheep drive into the "cool green pastures of the Sierras," John Muir wrote, after a day of sketching on North Dome Mountain, "No pain here, no dull empty hours, no fear of the past, no fear of the future. . . ."

So it is in November woods, or on November beaches. One is lulled into a sense of unchangingness. Siskins and chickadees work the cones together. A woodpecker knocks at intervals. Ducks settle into the cove. Gulls glide without effort. This is the way it was before the first man came. He would have been an Indian, in search of food or adventure. But before he came, what lived here? What grew? On a rainy night in late November I came back to the Island from a trip to town. Blot out the half-dozen home lights, and this is the way the Island would have looked to a lone approaching boatman—a long, dark, tree-enshrouded shape, a mystery, a challenge, perhaps a haven.

But the Island was old even then.

December

A Gathering of Shore Birds

Cormorants and ducks increased in numbers. A flock of bushtits, tiny, nondescript, gray-backed birds, worked over and under the remaining yellow leaves of the Gravenstein apple tree. Sheets of rain swept the water, and gray near the shore turned to green farther out. Gulls fought the wind, coasted back, and turned to climb the wind again, came in with a long free glide, making a game of the storm. Grebes with long white necks swam and dived or took off with drooping wings and a labored motion. Ducks sought sheltered waters. Some would remain all winter, others stopped only to feed and rest. Species intermingled and seemed to speak the same language. As I descended the trail to the cove I could hear their soft-voiced conversation, and I always tried to walk quietly, so as to take account of the various species. But one of them must have heard and given warning; for they all took off at once, gabbling, splashing, and treading water. They winged out and circled back as though to see whether I had gone, and then settled a little way offshore to wait me out.

The kingfisher chose to ignore my presence. His family had all gone, and he was alone again. He rolled in his orbit from limb to water and back to limb again. Wet sand at the end of the spit was thick with tracks, a marked map of hieroglyphics, a signed register—raccoon, deer, heron, hunter. The earth was littered with spent shell cases. No HUNTING signs were peppered with shot patterns. Someone had erected a crude blind and had killed and plucked his kill there. I found a mound of feathers, soft gray and the incredible blue of mallard spectrum. Once, on the sandspit, I came across a dead harlequin duck, a rare visitor to inland shores. I could only assume he had been shot out of curiosity by some trigger-happy sportsman attracted by his brilliant plumage.

High November tides ate daily into the bank of diatomaceous earth hard by the cove. Blocks made up of millions of microscopic skeletons of ancient diatoms with indestructible cell walls broke away and floated. Tunnels in the bank leading to the nest of the kingfisher and other species had been exposed by the erosion. One day a pigeon guillemot, still in summer plumage, started noisily from one of these, a black bird with bright red feet and white wing patches. Like the water ouzel, this big bank pigeon literally flies beneath the surface.

Cepphus columba, he goes, too, by the common name of guillemot pigeon. In flight, he made a strange reedy sound. Far out, a cormorant sat with wings widespread. There must have been a deadhead there, but he appeared to be sitting directly on the water. With his homely serpentine head, he looked as ancient as time itself. But the grebe, the true grebe, clowning in the cove, goes back to the Oligocene epoch, pre-man.

A story about grebes came to us in the papers. For centuries a colony of these historic birds had nested at Clear Lake, California. Fifteen years ago a chemical was sprayed over the lake in order to eliminate gnats that were annoying the inhabitants of a housing development. Having ingested fish that had ingested gnats, the grebes began to die. Their eggs failed to hatch. During five years' time only one grebe was seen in an area that had previously supported thousands. Lake waters turned murky and shores grew slimy with algae, a condition attributed to household nutrients seeping into the lake from septic systems. Smelt were introduced to eat the household nutrients, and the water cleared. When smelt began to grow too numerous, game fish were introduced to control the former. With the discontinuance of gnat spraying the grebes began to make a comeback. Never underestimate the ingenuity of man!

For some reason of his own, probably to do with protein content, a grebe eats his own feathers. He is an expert diver, with flaps along his toes that help him paddle, but his takeoff is awkward. He must taxi along the surface for several yards before becoming airborne. It is said that in the progressive flattening of a grebe's toe bones and in the long tibiotarsus and the short femur that form the leg joint, lie the entire thrilling story of evolution.

December Color

As the year wore away, colors became gentler and more muted. With the coming of occasional frost, the yellow of the goldenrod and of the still-blooming *Senecio* turned to a mustard shade. Wet leaf carpets changed from gold to russet, and twigs and boughs of conifers deepened to olive and avocado. Boles of madroñas browned to clove color, and spice shades prevailed, too, on husks of hardhack and ninebark and ocean spray. Coats of deer darkened to the tone of fir bark and brown cones blackened. Soft brown cat-tail heads stood above green ribbon leaves.

Beside the weathered water tower at Lizzie Larson's old place, a stump like a table top offered a banquet of burnt-orange mushrooms with pale yellow stems and gills of a strange exotic green. It is said that in Tierra del Fuego at the southern tip of South America, where food and water must be brought in over a hundred miles of distance, natives *live* largely on mushrooms, which have a high protein content with low calorie accumulation.

In the cove, the small gray water ouzel dipped and bobbed beside the stream and then went under, to emerge looking dry and resume his curtsying, as though in re-hearsal for a presentation. By mid-December the first van-guard of winter robins had begun to filter in, routing the cedar waxwings from the holly trees. The trees shook as though in a high wind, and by day's end most of the branches were stripped clean of berries.

When rain and wind ceased for a time, the open ex-panse of water with its changing streaks and pools of light and shadow was a continuous distraction. I have heard that Somerset Maugham, whose workroom faced the Medi-terranean, caused his windows to be boarded over so as not to be disturbed by the extensive panorama. A dozen times a day, weak and dilatory, I reach for the glasses, to watch a seal, a loon, a flock of ducks with bright, swol-len-looking bills, surf scoters driven in to the Sound by storms on the Pacific Ocean. A big freighter comes straight down the channel from The Narrows, but turns too far out for me to identify the flag. A wren visits each day to probe the leaves of evergreen clematis that fringe the front veranda. A kingfisher alights on a wild cherry seedling for a half hour's workout.

Purple and house finches swing on the fat basket and feed on the tray with rufous-sided towhees and the numerous juncos. Unable to gain a foothold, a Steller's jay leaps from branch to fat and back to branch again, keeping up an unearthly racket. The one-legged junco slopes in to the tray and lands, balanced neatly on his white-bordered tail feathers. The others tolerate him but accord him no special favors.

The total of daylight hours lessened and rain came again. The water turned olive green with long foamy whitecaps that piled mounds of froth on the beach, and floating deadheads bobbed to the surface and then disappeared, as though giant hands had drawn them under. A small black duck faced oncoming waves and dived as if for pleasure in the exercise. Frequently rain came at night, with a rushing sound against the windows. A comparative newcomer complained disconsolately of Island winters. "Summers are nice enough, but now the summer people are all gone and their houses are dark. . . ." "Days are too short here," she went on, forgetting that days are the same length on the mainland. She hated the sound of foghorns, and they *do* sound lonely. Perhaps you have to have a touch of melancholy in your disposition in order to like to hear them.

The Year's Shortest Day

A wind blew in from the northeast and piled up waves that crossed the road. Surf like ocean surf rolled in and brought logs, driftwood, and green and brown algae. Waters were empty of life on the surface save for two small ducks that kept close together and dived in unison, re-

maining down for a long time. Was it quiet and calm
down there? Even the spread-eagle cormorant was gone.

The gray windy sky was empty. Big waves broke with
a splashing sound and a guttural music of grinding and
sliding pebbles. On a log wedged against the bank, laced
with wild cucumber, rows of bracket fungi showed delicate
pink faces. Tiny chocolate-brown periwinkles, beached
when the tide receded, clung to pebbles by the hundreds.
It has been suggested that periwinkles may be gradually
becoming *land* animals.

Garrulous starlings held noisy conversations in rain-
dark trees. Their sharp bills, yellow last summer, had
darkened, and spots on their breasts were like pencil marks
on an English theme. On the ground, they swaggered.
They do not scare easily.

I went up into the woods to search for pink-stemmed
coral root I had seen in bloom there at midsummer. Even
at noon the wood was dark, without sound, vastly changed
with deciduous trees bare. I could not remember a strong
wind, but wind had blown there. I counted twenty trees
tipped against others, roots exposed and hung with black,
wet muck. The earth was as black as coal, soggy and satu-
rated. Nettle had seeded and seedlings stood six inches tall,
but had no sting. Buttercup mats spread in all directions.
Bright orange folded and twisted jelly fungi grew on wet
decaying logs, and patches of cream coral fungi, like tiny
branched shrubs, were everywhere. Silver leaves of foliose
lichen climbed black tree boles. I counted a dozen varieties
of lichen—little upstanding spoon shapes, flat crusts covered with shorthand, fans, shells, stars, blue-green, green-
blue, yellow, pink, gray, short orange threads, and long
gray beards—complex factories of fungi and algae living
together for mutual benefit. The word is *symbiosis*.

Deep cushions and mats of moss clothed all old fallen
logs. Some were topped by tiny bright red capsules. Even
the smallest fallen sticks were covered with clusters of ashy

polypores, thin, shell-like, overlapping brackets. Charred snags and stumps, head-high and filled with cavities and windows, stood like strange sculptured forms. Winter creeks flowed through flattened coarse grasses. Salamanders moved about with a sluggish motion.

The coral root was there. Stalks stood together in scaly clusters, strange leafless orchids without ability to manufacture chlorophyll. The name comes from the irregularly thickened roots that resemble coral. Fertilizing insects carry away sticky bits of flower on their heads, like little hats, or on proboscises, and so the species is continued.

However bleak the beach, the woods were little touched by winter. Fat red buds of broadleaf maple saplings showed diminutive tufts of bright green leaf beginnings. And the year not yet completed!

The Last Supper

On the final Sunday morning of the year I attended a nondenominational church service in the Island clubhouse. I had heard that the service was to be conducted by a young chaplain from Fort Lewis, on his way to Viet Nam, and went to see what he had to say about the debacle there. He did not mention Viet Nam. The service, rather, was a strange and moving celebration of the Eucharist, a simple breaking of Island bread together. We sat at a long table. A brown, homemade loaf went the rounds, followed by a stone pitcher. Each of us poured for his neighbor into the green coffee mugs we use for Island get-togethers.

The chaplain, whose name as I recall was John Snider, spoke quietly, of the way we push the meaningful aside for the trivial, the meaningless, and of how we set up golden calves of our own making. I had not seen John Snider (if, indeed, that was his name) prior to that morning. I have not seen or heard of him since. I do not know how he fared in Viet Nam, but I would like to know.

We awoke to a powdering of snow. The mainland was blotted out by snow squall. Boughs and leaves were lightly dusted, as though with powdered sugar. Cars left the Island piled with Christmas trees. I remembered for no reason a Christmas season in a Kansas rural school when we were unable to find a single suitable evergreen. We cut a persimmon, and children brought branches of prickly cedar from home yards. We tied them on with twine, and made chains from red and white crepe paper, strung popcorn and cranberries, and covered a star with tinsel.

The birds were ravenous. A purple finch dropped to the feeder with his heavily striped female. His suddenly lifted crest looked like reverse-brushed nap of wine velvet. The pair was joined by an orange and black towhee, his color intensified by snow. A swirl of gray and black juncos came. And then a flash of blue, a Steller's jay.

Each night a raccoon climbed to the feeding board nailed to the outside window sill. We sat at the lighted table and watched him pick and choose among the crusts of bread. He prefers bread to grain, and fat to either. When a smaller raccoon came creeping up through the rhododendron, he warned it away with a growl. Having cleaned up every crumb, he hunched away, hyena-shaped, pausing now and then to look back over his shoulder.

A sheet of ice sheathed the birdbath, but juncos must have their bath no matter what the weather. They stomped and skated. The sun came out and shone on Mount Rainier, sparkling white from top to bottom. The peak wore a white cloud cap shaped like a zeppelin, but with wind-whipped edges.

A solitary crow alighted in the cottonwood and called at intervals in a coaxing, uncrowlike manner, his voice soft and oddly appealing. Was he a Northwestern crow, *Corvus caurinus,* said to be smaller, with a voice more resonant? Not one of his fellows came, or answered. He sat with a dejected droop, like some outcast from the tribe. On Jacobs Point there is a rookery, a communal roost; feeding crows post a watch. But here we see them only in passing. They may pause in the top branches of the cottonwood and fill the air with raucous cawing, but they are soon gone. We rarely see a loner. This one sat throughout the afternoon, speaking now and then in soft tones, then flapped away. His notched wings were like pointing fingers.

I remembered the crow heads and crow eggs upon which a bounty was paid at the Montgomery County courthouse when I was a child. Did I really help to collect and to count the bloody heads in the bloody sacks, to share in the spoils? *Spoils* was the word; they smelled to high heaven. We robbed nests without compunction. Expendable crows settled by hundreds on squat dark tepees of corn shocks in winter.

A few ravens live on the Island, big purple-black, rowdy-looking passerines that have no necks or shoulders. Their call is a hoarse croak, "Nevermore!" They walk about the mud flats on Oro Bay when the tide is out and eat dead fish, dead crabs, dead most anything. They look like indigent old ladies dressed in black and picking over garbage.

Orange-banded woolly bears undulated across the road, caterpillars of Isabella moths, the gold moths with spotted abdomens we had seen in early autumn. Awkward and overdressed, they lumbered, like students in coonskin coats. Had the mild winter confused their timetable? Did they think spring had come? They fed on still green plantain leaves. Old-timers say that the width of black span on a woolly bear foretells the severity of coming weather.

Shed hairs are used by the larva to spin silk for egg-shaped cocoons in which pupae sleep until the moths emerge. Disturbed woolly bears roll into black and orange balls for protection, or to feign death. They look soft and beautiful but they feel unpleasant, like bristles on a harsh brush.

Fence barbs were matted with deer hair that would be used in nest-building come spring. Deer creep through or under fences unless pursued. Then they sail over. On mild nights, a few frogs raised hoarse voices in the swamp. Were they, too, deceived? We heard the solitary song of frog, or toad, underneath the floor. Unlike the rousing chorus of early spring, frog voices in winter sound sleepy.

The old and lovely dogwood along the drive is dying. Only a trace of life near the top of the crown remains. But new dogwoods are coming. The king is dead. Long live the king. The little hawk likes to sit among the dead limbs, high up, to watch for movement. His eyes look blood red in the light. Children and grownups walk along the roads with measuring sticks, searching for the perfect Christmas tree. There are so many it is difficult to choose.

Christmas Day, so long anticipated, was mild and fair, too springlike for Christmas. People said, "We'll pay in January." Pussy willow buds were swollen. Brought inside, they opened in a few hours and took on a soft gray color with pink overtones. Mountains on either side looked white and cold, but water reflected a sky of Wedgwood blue.

Once Christmas is under way, spring seems to wait just beyond the next milepost. Taking stock in the yard, I found lavender primroses in bloom among the crinkled leaves, and flowers of yellow jasmine, cherry *autumnalis*, pale purple heather, and flame and gold calendulas. A package labeled "Oklahoma holly" arrived from a cherished friend in Oklahoma, where I made my home for twenty years.

Out came a seed pod from trumpet creeper, a rough green Osage orange "hedge apple," and four strange split-beaked devil's claws, cross-hatched seed capsules of wild unicorn plant, *Martynia louisiana,* with pointed, bearded tongues extruded. Unicorn capsules open longitudinally, to form themselves into long claws curved like the horns of bighorn sheep, and so catch free rides in the hair of passing animals.

At the bottom of the box, carefully wrapped in tissue, lay a small sheaf of golden heads of winter wheat. Christmas, more than any other season, jogs the memory. The smell and sight of that ripe wheat, perfectly preserved somehow from summer harvest, brought a flood of recollections.

Midnight on the Beach

A few days after Christmas I had as guests two of my young Kansas nieces and their husbands. The girls have always showed a keen interest in anything pertaining to science and the out-of-doors, and so we paid a midnight visit to the cove. The tide stood at a minus three, and a pale moon gave to the receded water a silver sheen; but the beach and sandspit made up a no-man's land, a chilly, damp expanse of mystery.

A smell of salt, iodine, and mud came from the emptied cove, an odor that, in twenty years, has become a fragrance. A raccoon, disturbed at his beachcombing, melted away into the shadows, and we heard the soft rustle of a deer's departure. Flashlights revealed masses of yellow snail eggs like grains of wheat, exposed on intertidal boulders. A dozen varieties of limpets clung to wet stones. Listening, we were surrounded by squirts and pops and splashes made by a myriad of living creatures underneath the surface.

Near low-water line we found more starfishes in number and color than I have seen anywhere at one time save on the shores of Pender Harbor in British Columbia Province. A big sunflower star boasted twenty-two rays, two more than normal. The blood stars, with long tapering rays, shone blood red and shades of deep and bright orange. A purple-brown leather star lived up to its name, with a leather texture. Where a small, thick-rayed star with a humped disk had lost an arm, a new one had started. It is said that members of one starfish family, *Linckia*, can regenerate an entire animal from a single remaining appendage.

With their petal-like rays and vivid shades and colors, these many sea stars made of the beach a fascinating flower garden. Sun stars were blue-gray, with rays ten to twelve in number. We turned a few, to examine the grooves and tube feet on the ventral sides, and admired the muscle control as the animals quickly reversed position, using their arms as levers. We rescued a clam from one specimen that held the bivalve in a death embrace. Some starfish feed on shellfish, barnacles, and crabs by taking the entire animal into the stomach and discharging the shells in a later action. Others extrude their stomachs to ingest and digest their victims. Held by an arm, the starfish literally squeezes out water, though more slowly than the moon snail, and becomes ounces lighter. I am still in search of an explanation as to why we saw so many more sea stars at midnight than I have seen by day at even lower ebb-tide levels.

Over and Out

On the last day of the year we awoke to snow. Snow had fallen silently throughout a windless night, and the air was thick with big flakes, the earth obscured. The frustrated cats leapt and almost sank from sight. Robins floundered to the feeder for cut apple and took off in a flurry of wet snow, but juncos ran lightly over the surface, their black cloaks feathered with white shoulder pieces.

A musky smell of mink, stronger and more unpleasant than remembered civet, came up into the wood closet from underneath the house, and we discovered the tracks, neat little double prints that came up from the beach and ended beyond the rock wall, the terminus of an old drain-box tunnel that crossed the yard from the house foundation. The mercury plummeted to twenty, an unusual low for this vicinity. Clouds of steam arose from the channel, and when the wind blew, an occasional vapor "tornado," not unlike the traveling dust devils in Kansas and Oklahoma fields, sped across the surface of the water.

The few roses still bravely blooming were encased in ice, like flowers imprisoned in plastic eardrops. Cedars turned to silver lace. A purple finch sang a few liquid notes from the depths of a holly tree. All birds ate feverishly, as though they never expected to eat again.

Snow turned to sleet and then to freezing rain, and roads glazed over. Under their burden of ice, trees made groaning sounds as if in pain, and icicles knocked from eaves shattered with noises like glass breaking. We hurried to fill and clean the kerosene lamps and lanterns. An ice-burdened tree might well fall across a power line. The lamps give off a mellow light, and we rather hoped to use them. But because of the whiteness of the snow, darkness was a long time coming. Power had not failed and so we turned out the lights and sat by firelight. Windows reflected the red of leaping flames, and lights on the mainland looked far away. The year was dying on the Island and to the west, over the Pacific Ocean. We spoke of New Year's fireworks watched, once, from a hill above the city of Honolulu, an unforgettable experience. On the East Coast of the United States the New Year had already begun and revelers had ended their festivities.

A decade was dying, too, a decade during which man had set foot on the moon but during which he had also become suddenly and sharply aware of his own precarious position on this planet, his only home, his only star.

"Twelve o'clock," someone reminded. We opened the door to look and listen. Something should happen, surely.

An old man with a scythe should materialize from the snow and take off into night sky or a little snow image should come running up the road. But nothing of the sort occurred. From the muted radio behind us, or from across dark water, came, real or imagined, the sound of whistles and of bells, and the year was over.

RAPE

The wilderness erodes. What remains of it survives in isolated and glorious patches, on mountainsides and remote islands and dark swamps and deserts. . . . The wilderness erodes. And as it does, perhaps we do too. . . .*

So far as is known, the first permanent settler, Christian Christensen, reached Anderson Island shores about the year 1870.

During a century of slow settlement, man and nature lived together here in symbiotic harmony, each taking according to need and giving in turn. Trees were harvested, clearing accomplished, to warm, feed, and shelter families. The community expanded, as have thousands of communities, in a leisurely fashion, closely knit, isolated, self-reliant, and content. Save for a brief interlude of brick-making from local clay, a kind of folk art that engendered a small population impetus, the Island remained essentially agricultural.

A few subdivisions occurred—Villa Beach, along the east shore, Miller and Dunkel's and Thorlands, in the vicinity of Amsterdam Bay, the waterfronts we call "Little Burien" and "Mailman's Point." But these were acreages. Our own plat in Villa Beach, purchased in 1950, comprises some

* Donald Jackson, "Threatened America," *Life*, 1 August 1969.

seven acres. An occasional "second home" was built. Several buyers, as we did, settled into old houses no longer occupied. We were summer people, week-enders. We made little impact.

Although privately owned, the big lakes area on a high bluff in the eastern sector retained its wild character, as did most of the central portion—the swamp and its tributaries, the woods, the several gulches. Abandoned farms reverted, and were lost in growth. The lakes area was a haven for wild fowl and deer, a territory of bald eagles, great blue heron, great horned owl, pileated woodpecker, and all manner of smaller birds. Islanders took huckleberries and blackberries, greens, fuel, fish, an occasional venison, wild ducks in migration. The road in was an unimproved trail through brush and trees.

A few years ago, at one end of Lake Josephine, a small project began. A little clearing was made, lots were surveyed and staked. Three or four modest buildings materialized. But the long road in, past the Island cemetery, remained little more than a wide path choked with bracken and blackberry and alder seedlings, winding through woods and underbrush and turning aside for big trees, as had the first roads on the Island. Efforts to construct a year-around switchback from the high bluff to the beach failed because of springs and seeps in winter.

The first flurry of trepidation subsided. With the owner's consent and knowledge, Islanders continued to look upon most of the lakes area as more or less open range, as they had always done.

Only when change comes swiftly does one feel its full impact. During these past three years Island woods have undergone more "erosion" than any of us would have believed possible. Roads that were little more than lanes have been widened to accommodate heavy traffic and smoothed to allow for (and, incidentally, to encourage) speed. Acres upon acres of woods, comprising approximately one-fifth of the Island land mass, have been surveyed, mapped, platted into small lots, infiltrated by a latticed network of wide slashed roads that go nowhere. One broad section of beautiful trees has been replaced by a parklike, well-kept, privately owned golf course and a landscaped "country club."

In a recent effort to come at some kind of estimate of the mileage entailed, we drove over a few of these roads, checking and making notes. Linkages proved so frequent, "Drives," "Lanes," "Places," "Circles," and cul-de-sacs so numerous and so engineered, that we gave up long before we had exhausted the mileage on the first project. Even so, the sum of our notations was scarcely credible.

The Island remains, of course, as it has always been, a good place to live. Islanders are a hospitable as well as an adaptable people. Now that Lake Josephine and all of the surrounding acres are "project," they no longer trespass. The few buyers who have come to make their homes in the area are welcomed in community affairs. The island is not bridged to the mainland. There are, as yet, no overnight facilities, no restaurants, no taverns, no movie houses. There is still a feeling of isolation, a strong sense of community. We have not yet reached the status of a suburban development with scattered interests. But we may well do so.

When half of Lake Florence, too, was taken over, an effort (as yet unsuccessful) was made to secure at least a small portion of the lake for public swimming. Prices that the developers have set on lake-front lots remain, so far, prohibitive.

Meanwhile, the creeping destruction continues. Hundreds of acres have been added. Woods have been bulldozed, chain-sawed, segmented into thousands of building lots. Miles upon miles of rocked roads have opened woods that were once a natural preserve for native fauna and flora. Marsh and swamp have been invaded, fills made and drain tiles laid to create more land for profitable segmentation.

Given half an opportunity in this temperate climate, healing sets in at a rapid rate. As I have pointed out, some shoots, some roots, will penetrate asphalt to reach light, air, soil, if need be. Much wildlife, too, such as deer, raccoons, and chipmunks, adapts to man's poor ways. If they are fed, raccoons and chipmunks and sometimes deer become so cheeky as hardly to merit the name of wildlife.

The loss will be among the shy, the scarce, the timid— pileated and downy woodpeckers, band-tailed pigeons, cedar waxwings, the hermit thrush, the dusky horned owl, the bald eagle, the great blue heron. The loss of flora, of "little lives," cannot be estimated. Kinnikinnick and twin-flower are readily killed and do not replace themselves. The admission of light does away with such as coral root, mahonia, and rattlesnake plantain, to which shade is a necessity for survival. Many species of fauna—chickadee, owl, woodpecker, nuthatch, creeper, wren, flycatcher—cannot thrive without the stumps and snags that provide food and nesting sites, stumps and snags that have, with the help of truckloads of discarded tires, undergone cremation. The wilderness erodes.

To clear shore lines for swimming and boat-launching, an underwater mower is kept at work clipping wild iris, cattails, and pond lilies. Interlocking roads are widened still further by "frontage roads," kept clean of growth by busy scrapers—mile upon mile upon mile of parking strips. The building of one wide roadway, of a single golf course, may well result in the elimination of a species in an area with a natural barricade such as an island.

Although few houses have gone up around the lakes as yet, Lake Josephine is already altered to the point where many swimmers fear to enter. Whether because of fertilizer runoff from the small well-kept lawns and park sites that touch the shore line and the golf course that adjoins the water-side country club grounds, or from some other cause, a deep algal slime now carpets the lake floor. Only a few years ago water from either lake was sufficiently clean for house use. By the summer of 1971 Lake Josephine was murky and filled with stinking debris. In the vicinity of the diving raft, a floating rainbow of oil (some say from the busy underwater mower) coated the once-sparkling surface that Michael Luark described, aptly, as a mirror for trees and sky.

Should homes arise on lots already sold, hundreds of septic systems will surround the lakes. Although test-holes were required at intervals on all land platted in order to determine filtration, no sewer line nor treatment plant was provided for. One engineer experienced in development problems faced too late remarked sadly, "It will be a sea of sewage." How much pollution can the earth tolerate?

"Prospects in the hands of a well-briefed salesman are a queer lot," he mused. "They'll buy a little parcel on which to build a house, without seeming to notice the network of stakes that mark several hundred other parcels. By the time they've cleared sufficient space to build a house and carport, bury a septic tank, lay out a drainfield and a parking area, and their neighbors do likewise, there won't be any woods left."

"We only bought our lot as investment," some say. "I will argue," wrote Sylvia Porter, syndicated columnist of *Your Money's Worth,* "with touting these tiny parcels as a great 'investment.' There are millions of land parcels on the market today, so scarcity certainly won't be a factor driving up prices in the foreseeable future. In many cases all of the 'investment' value . . . and then some . . . is being reaped by the developers."

Regrettable as it seems to have opened the lakes area to these profitable bits, the invasion of the swamp, nurse-ground to a variety of life, is perhaps the more damaging. The swamp teems with life. Once unknown save to Island-ers and to the occasional passerby in winter who may have caught a glimpse of seasonal water through defoliated trees, woods leading to the swamp have become a potential suburbia.

Rocked roads have been cut through as far as the terrain would allow and labeled with street names. Roads parallel each other or run in neat artistic curves. Mobile homes and trailers occupy a developed camping site. Wheels and blades have scraped away elder bushes, blackcap, hardhack, and huckleberry. One evening in early spring I trespassed past rows of numbered stakes and sleeping earth-movers. Crushed salamanders, caught in migration, lay in the roadway. The air was filled with the smell and the presence of wood smoke, pitch fragrance of conifers that smoldered in heaps in clearings from which stumps had been blasted, the slightly bitter smell of burning madroña.

Depressed by damp air, smoke hung trapped in the woods and stood in a blue-gray pall over the stagnant water. The swamp had lost the brooding mystery that gave it distinction. The entire character of the place was changed. Whatever the incalculable loss to wildlife, the *human* race has lost something, too.

Some predict, hopefully, that the urban density of building will be a long time in coming, citing building costs and Island inaccessibility. But, open and enticing as they are, these woods will be trampled by those who fail to notice the small, the seemingly insignificant forms of life, or by those who simply attach ᴸo value to such. Nor can a bulldozer stop for a clump of coral root which the operator in all probability cannot see. Who could expect a machine as big as a house to turn aside for a salamander?

I do not reject the fact that the time has come when we must share our space. The human population of the earth, this state, the county is on the increase. On the ferry one day I heard a salesman remark to a prospect, "The Islanders have had *their* way long enough." I assume he meant *human* Islanders. Perhaps he is right. How do you reply to accusations of selfishness, of wanting things *your* way, of a pig-headed reluctance to share?

Were we to parcel the Island (a hypothetical solution) into ten- or even five-acre tracts, served by county roads already in existence, many more inhabitants than we currently support could enjoy the wildness with a minimum of damage to other species. We would still be a community instead of a conglomerate.

It has been said that when roads open up the land it is permanently gone. Nature suffers defeat under tons of crushed rock. And then there are the "little roads" that wend their way picturesquely into the woods between each segment of lots—trails and paths that, given a bit of slope, become silt-carrying freshets.

Anderson Island is no Grand Canyon, no Everglades, no redwood forest, to arouse public indignation. It is only one of the "little wild places," one endangered island in Puget Sound. But great losses are made up of small losses. We can not shrug this off as *progress*. Nor is it just we who have lost. America has been deprived. Our children and our children's children have been cheated out of that wildness that should have been their heritage.

List of Plant Names

Note: Where I have found discrepancies in guidebooks concerning scientific names of plants listed, I have used E. L. D. Seymour, *The Wise Garden Encyclopedia* (New York: Grosset and Dunlap, 1970), as authority. No scientific names have been included for fungi, algae, or lichens. The letters spp. indicate the existence of several species of the same genus.

COMMON NAME	SCIENTIFIC NAME
Ageratum (flossflower)	*Ageratum nanum*
Alder, western red	*Alnus rubra*
Alumroot	
Small-flower	*Heuchera micrantha*
Oval-leaf	*Heuchera ovalifolia*
Anise	*Pimpinella anisum*
Ash	
Oregon	*Fraxinus oregona*
Mountain	*Sorbus* spp.
Aster (Michaelmas daisy)	*Aster douglasii*
Balsamroot, northwest	*Balsamorhiza deltoidea*
Baneberry	*Actaea arguta*
Baptisia (wild indigo)	*Baptisia vespertina*
Bedstraw	
Northern	*Galium boreale*
Annual	*Galium aparine*

Common Name	Scientific Name
Bishop's cap (mitrewort)	*Mitella* spp.
Bittersweet	*Celastrus scandens*
Blackberry	
Trailing	*Rubus macropetalus*
Oregon evergreen	*Rubus laciniatus*
Himalaya	*Rubus procerus*
Blackcap (black raspberry)	*Rubus leucodermis*
Bleeding heart	*Dicentra formosa*
Blue-eyed grass	*Sisyrinchium inflatum*
Blue sailors (chicory)	*Cichorium intybus*
Bracken fern	*Pteridium aquilinum*
Brooklime (speedwell)	*Veronica americana*
Broom, Scotch	*Cytisus scoparius*
Buttercup	
Western	*Ranunculus occidentalis*
Creeping	*Ranunculus repens*
Bongard's	*Ranunculus bongardii*
Calendula	*Calendula* spp.
California poppy	*Eschscholzia californica*
Camas, death	*Zigadenus venenosus*
Cascara (buckthorn)	*Rhamnus purshiana*
Catclaw sensitive briar	*Schrankia uncinata*
Cat's ear, hairy	*Hypochaeris radicata*
Cat-tail	*Typha latifolia*
Cedar, western red	*Thuja plicata*
Chamomile (dog fennel or stinking Mayweed)	*Anthemis arvensis*
Cherry	
Bitter (wild)	*Prunus emarginata*
Winter-blooming ornamental	*Prunus autumnalis*
Chickweed, field	*Cerastium arvense*
Chicory (blue sailors; succory)	*Cichorium intybus*
Cinquefoil	*Potentilla gracilis*
Clematis	*Clematis* spp.
Collomia	*Collomia grandiflora*

COMMON NAME	SCIENTIFIC NAME
Coltsfoot (butterbur)	*Petasites speciosa*
Columbine	
Western	*Aquilegia formosa*
Blue	*Aquilegia coerulea*
Compass plant	*Wyethia angustifolia*
Coneflower	*Lepachys pulcherrima*
Convolvulus (bindweed)	*Convolvulus* spp.
Coral root	*Corallorhiza maculata*
Cornel, dwarf (bunchberry)	*Cornus canadensis*
Corydalis, golden	*Corydalis aurea*
Cotoneaster	*Cotoneaster* spp.
Cottonwood	*Populus trichocarpa*
Crabapple, Pacific	*Pyrus diversifolia*
Crocus	*Crocus* spp.
Cucumber, wild	*Echinocystis oreganus*
Currant, red-flower	*Ribes sanguineum*
Daffodil	*Narcissus pseudo-narcissus*
Daisy	
Oxeye	*Chrysanthemum leucanthemum*
English	*Dellis perennis*
Death camas	*Zigadenus venenosus*
Deer fern	*Struthiopteris spicant*
Devil's claws (unicorn plant)	*Martynia louisiana*
Dock	*Rumex* spp.
Dodder	*Cuscuta salina*
Dog-tooth violet	*Erythronium oregonum*
Dogwood	
Pacific	*Cornus nuttallii*
Red-osier	*Cornus stolonifera*
Dutchman's breeches	*Dicentra cucullaria*
Elder	
Blue-berry	*Sambucus glauca*
Red-berry	*Sambucus callicarpa*
Black-berry	*Sambucus melanocarpa*
Everlasting, pearly	*Anaphalis margaritacea*

Common Name	Scientific Name
Fairy bells, Oregon	*Disporum oreganum*
Fig	*Ficus* spp.
Filbert (hazelnut)	*Corylus* spp.
Fir, Douglas	*Pseudotsuga taxifolia*
Firethorn	*Pyracantha* spp.
Fireweed (blooming Sally)	*Epilobium augustifolium*
Flax, wild	*Linum lewisii*
Fleabane, large purple	*Erigeron speciosus*
Foam flower	*Tiarella unifoliata*
Forsythia	*Forsythia* spp.
Foxglove	*Digitalis purpurea*
Fringe cup	*Tellima parviflora*
Fritillary (rice root lily)	*Fritillaria camschatcensis*
Gaillardia (Indian blanket flower)	*Gaillardia pulchella*
Geranium, wild	*Geranium viscosissimum*
Ginger, wild	*Asarum caudatum*
Goatsbeard	*Aruncus sylvester*
Goldenrod	*Solidago* spp.
Gooseberry, wild	*Ribes divaricatum*
Grape, wild	*Vitis* spp.
Gumweed	*Grindelia squarrosa*
Hackberry	*Celtis douglasii*
Hardhack (steeple bush)	*Spiraea douglasii*
Hawthorn, English	*Crataegus oxyacantha*
Hazel	*Corylus californica*
Heal-all (self-heal)	*Prunella vulgaris*
Heather	*Calluna* spp.
Hemlock	*Tsuga heterophylla*
Holly	*Ilex* spp.
Honestie (moonwort; satin flower)	*Lunaria annua*
Honeysuckle	
Orange	*Lonicera ciliosa*
Blue fly	*Lonicera caerulea*
Purple	*Lonicera hispidula*
Twinberry	*Lonicera involucrata*

COMMON NAME	SCIENTIFIC NAME
Horsechestnut	*Aesculus hippocastanum*
Horsetail	*Equisetum arvense*
Huckleberry	
Evergreen	*Vaccinium ovatum*
Red	*Vaccinium parvifolium*
Indian paintbrush	*Castilleja miniata*
Indian plum (oso-berry)	*Osmaronia cerasiformis*
Jacob's ladder	*Polemonium humile*
Jasmine	*Jasminum* spp.
Johnny-jump-up	*Viola* spp.
Kentucky coffee (coffee bean)	*Gymnocladus dioica*
Kinnikinnick (bearberry)	*Arctostaphylos uva-ursi*
Laburnum (goldenchain)	*Laburnum* spp.
Lady fern	*Athyrium filix-femina*
Larkspur	
Plains	*Delphinium virescens*
Rock	*Delphinium tricorne*
Licorice fern	*Polypodium vulgare*
Lily	
Calla	*Zantedeschia* spp.
Wild tiger (wood)	*Lilium parviflorum*
Yellow pond	*Nymphaea polysepala*
Locust	*Robinia pseudo-acacia*
Lupine	*Lupinus* spp.
Madroña	*Arbutus menziesii*
Mahonia (Oregon grape)	*Berberis aquifolium*
	Berberis nervosa
Maidenhair fern	*Adiantum pedatum*
Mallow, musk	*Malva moschata*
Maple	
Broadleaf	*Acer macrophyllum*
Douglas	*Acer glabrum*
Vine	*Acer circinatum*
Miner's lettuce	*Claytonia perfoliata*
Siberian	*Claytonia sibirica*
Mint, Canada	*Mentha canadensis*
Mitrewort	*Mitella ovalis*

COMMON NAME	SCIENTIFIC NAME
Mock orange	*Philadelphia gordonianus*
Monkey flower, yellow	*Mimulus langsdorfii*
Monkshood	*Aconitum columbianum*
Montbretia	*Tritonia crocata*
Mountain ash	*Sorbus* spp.
Mountain balm (sticky laurel)	*Ceanothus velutinus*
Mustard	*Brassica* spp.
Narcissus, poet's	*Narcissus poeticus*
Nasturtium	*Tropaeolum majus*
Nettle	
Hedge	*Stachys ciliata*
Stinging	*Urtica lyallii*
Ninebark	*Physocarpus capitatus*
Oak	
Garry	*Quercus garryana*
Poison	*Rhus diversiloba*
Ocean spray	*Holodiscus discolor*
Oregon grape, tall	*Berberis aquifolium*
	Berberis nervosa
Osage orange	*Maclura pomifera*
Oso-berry (Indian plum)	*Osmaronia cerasiformis*
Owl's clover	*Orthocarpus bracteosus*
Oyster plant	
Yellow	*Tragopogon pratensis*
Purple	*Tragopogon porrifolius*
Papaw	*Asimina triloba*
Pasqueflower	*Anemone patens*
Western	*Anemone occidentalis*
Pea, many-leafed	*Lathyrus polyphyllus*
Pearly everlasting	*Anaphalis margaritacea*
Penstemon (beardtongue)	*Penstemon* spp.
Persimmon	*Diospyros virginiana*
Philodendron	*Philodendron* spp.
Pickleweed (samphire)	*Salicornia* spp.
Pine, lodgepole (jackpine)	*Pinus contorta*
Pipsissewa	*Chimaphila umbellata*

Common Name	Scientific Name
Plum, wild	*Prunus* spp.
Poison ivy	*Rhus toxicodendron*
Polygonum	
Knotweed	*Polygonum bistortoides*
Water buckwheat	*Polygonum amphibium*
Primrose	*Primula* spp.
Pussywillow	*Salix discolor*
Queen Anne's lace (wild carrot)	*Daucus carota*
Ragweed	*Ambrosia* spp.
Ragwort, golden	*Senecio jacobaea*
Raspberry, wild (blackcap)	*Rubus leucodermis*
Rattlesnake plantain	*Peramium decipiens*
Rhododendron, wild	*Rhododendron albiflorum*
Rose, wild	*Rosa* spp.
Rudbeckia	*Rudbeckia hirta*
Rush, scouring	*Equisetum hyemale*
St. Johnswort	*Hypericum perforatum*
Salal	*Gaultheria shallon*
Salmonberry	*Rubus spectabilis*
Samphire (pickleweed)	*Salicornia subterminalis*
Sedge	*Carex* spp.
Serviceberry (shadbush)	*Amelanchier florida*
Silverweed	*Potentilla anserina*
Skunk cabbage	*Lysichitum americanum*
Snapdragon	*Antirrhinum* spp.
Snowberry (waxberry)	*Symphoricarpos albus*
Snowdrop	*Galanthus nivalis*
Solomon's seal, star-flowered	*Smilacina stellata*
Sorrel	
Yellow wood	*Oxalis suksdorfii*
Sheep (redweed)	*Rumex acetosella*
Wood, pink	*Oxalis oregana*
Spiderwort	*Tradescantia canaliculata*
Spring gold	*Lomatium utriculatum*
Star flower	*Trientalis latifolia*

Common Name	Scientific Name
Storksbill	*Erodium cicutarium*
Strawberry, wild	*Fragaria bracteata*
Strawflower	*Helichrysum bracteatum*
Sword fern	*Polystichum munitum*
Sycamore (buttonwood)	*Platanus occidentalis*
Tansy	*Tanacetum vulgare*
Teasel	*Dipsacus sylvestris*
Thimbleberry	*Rubus parviflorus*
Thistle	
Common	*Cirsium lanceolatum*
Canada	*Cirsium arvensis*
Edible	*Cirsium edule*
Toadflax, ivy-leaved	*Cymbalaria muralis*
Trillium, western (wake robin)	*Trillium ovatum*
Tritoma (red-hot poker)	*Kniphofia uvaria*
Trout lily	*Erythronium oregonum*
Trumpet-creeper	*Campsis radicans*
Twinberry	*Lonicera involucrata*
Twinflower	*Linnaea borealis*
Twisted stalk	*Streptopus amplexifolius*
Unicorn	*Martynia louisiana*
Vanilla leaf	*Achlys triphylla*
Vetch	*Vicia gigantea*
Violet	
Blue	*Viola adunca*
Trailing yellow	*Voila sempervirens*
Yellow	*Viola glabella*
Wake robin	*Trillium ovatum*
Walnut, English	*Juglans regia*
Water crowfoot buttercup	*Ranunculus aquatilis*
Willow	
Pussy	*Salix discolor*
Pacific	*Salix lasiandra*
Yarrow	*Achillea millefolium*
Youth-on-age (pick-a-back)	*Tolmiea menziesi*

List of Bird Names

Common Name	Scientific Name
Auklet	
Cassin's	*Ptychoramphus aleuticus*
Rhinoceros	*Cerorhinca monocerata*
Bittern, American	*Botaurus lentiginosus*
Blackbird	
Red-winged	*Agelaius phoeniceus*
Brewer's	*Euphagus cyanocephalus*
Bluebird	*Sialia mexicana*
Bobwhite	*Colinus virginianus*
Brant, black	*Branta nigricans*
Bushtit, common	*Psaltriparus minimus*
Butcher bird (shrike)	*Lanius ludovicianus*
Cardinal	*Richmondena cardinalis*
Catbird	*Dumetella carolinensis*
Chickadee	
Black-capped	*Parus atricapillus*
Chestnut-backed	*Parus rufescens*
Cormorant	
Baird's	*Phalacrocorax pelagicus*
Brandt's	*Phalacrocorax penicillatus*
Cowbird, brown-headed	*Molothrus ater*
Creeper, California	*Certhia familiaris*
Crow, western	*Corvus brachyrhynchos*

239

COMMON NAME	SCIENTIFIC NAME
Cuckoo, yellow-billed	*Coccyzus americanus*
Dipper (water ouzel)	*Cinclus mexicanus*
Duck	
Baldpate	*Mareca americana*
Buffle-head	*Bucephala albeola*
Canvas-back	*Aythya valisineria*
Goldeneye, common	*Bucephala clangula*
Harlequin	*Histrionicus histrionicus*
Mallard, common	*Anas platyrhynchos*
Merganser, American	*Mergus merganser*
Merganser, hooded	*Lophodytes cucullatus*
Merganser, red-breasted	*Mergus serrator*
Old squaw	*Clangula hyemalis*
Pintail	*Anas acuta*
Red-head	*Aythya americana*
Scaup, greater	*Aythya marila*
Scaup, lesser	*Aythya affinis*
Scoter, common	*Oidemia nigra*
Scoter, surf	*Melanitta perspicillata*
Scoter, white-winged	*Melanitta deglandi*
Shoveller	*Spatula clypeata*
Teal, green-winged	*Anas carolinensis*
Widgeon, American	*Mareca americana*
Wood	*Aix sponsa*
Eagle	
Bald	*Haliaeetus leucocephalus*
Golden	*Aquila chrysaetos*
Finch	
Purple	*Carpodacus purpureus*
House	*Carpodacus mexicanus*
Flicker, red-shafted	*Colaptes cafer*
Flycatcher	
Traill's	*Empidonax traillii*
Western	*Empidonax difficilis*
Olive-sided	*Nuttallornis borealis*
Goldfinch	*Spinus tristis*

COMMON NAME	SCIENTIFIC NAME
Goose	
Cackling	*Branta canadensis*
Lesser snow	*Chen hyperborea*
Goshawk	*Accipiter gentilis*
Grebe	
Holboell's	*Colymbus grisegena*
Horned	*Colymbus auritus*
Eared	*Podiceps caspicus*
Western	*Aechmophorus occidentalis*
Grosbeak	
Black-headed	*Pheucticus melanocephalus*
Evening, western	*Hesperiphona vespertina*
Grouse	
Blue	*Dendragapus obscurus*
Oregon ruffed	*Bonasa umbellus*
Guillemot pigeon (sea pigeon)	*Cepphus columba*
Gull	
Glaucous-winged	*Larus glaucescens*
Western	*Larus occidentalis*
Herring	*Larus argentatus*
California	*Larus californicus*
Ring-billed	*Larus delawarensis*
Mew	*Larus canus*
Bonaparte's	*Larus philadelphia*
Hawk	
Sharp-shinned	*Accipiter velox*
Cooper's	*Accipiter cooperi*
Western red-tailed	*Accipiter buteo borealis*
Heron, great blue	*Ardea herodias*
Hummingbird, rufous	*Selasphorus rufus*
Jay	
Steller's	*Cyanocitta stelleri*
Oregon	*Perisoreus obscurus*
Junco, Oregon	*Junco hyemalis*
Killdeer	*Charadrius vociferus*
Kingfisher, western belted	*Megaceryle alcyon*

Common Name	Scientific Name
Kinglet, golden-crowned	*Regulus satrapa*
Loon	
Lesser	*Gavia immer*
Pacific	*Gavia arctica*
Red-throated	*Gavia stellata*
Martin, purple	*Progne subis*
Meadowlark, western	*Sturnella neglecta*
Murre, California	*Uria aalge*
Murrelet, marbled	*Brachyramphus marmoratus*
Nighthawk, Pacific	*Chordeiles minor*
Nuthatch, red-breasted	*Sitta canadensis*
Osprey	*Pandion haliaetus*
Owl	
Screech	*Asio otus*
Dusky horned	*Bubo virginianus*
Coast pygmy	*Glaucidium gnoma*
Short-eared	*Asio flammeus*
Saw-whet	*Aegolius acadicus*
Snowy	*Nyctea nyctea*
Pelican, white	*Pelecanus erythrorhynchos*
Pheasant, ring-necked	*Phasianus colchicus*
Pigeon	
Band-tailed	*Columba fasciata*
Guillemot (sea)	*Cepphus columba*
Quail, California	*Lophortyx californica*
Raven, American	*Corvus corax*
Robin, Northwestern	*Turdus migratorius*
Sanderling	*Crocethia alba*
Sandpiper	
Spotted	*Actitis macularia*
Least ("peep")	*Erolia minutilla*
Shrike (butcher bird)	*Lanius ludovicianus*
Siskin, northern pine	*Spinus pinus*
Snipe, common	*Capella gallinago*
Solitaire, Townsend's	*Myadestes townsendi*
Sparrow	
Western chipping	*Spizella passerina*

COMMON NAME	SCIENTIFIC NAME
Puget Sound white-crowned	*Zonotrichia leucophrys*
Golden-crowned	*Zonotrichia atricapilla*
Sooty fox	*Passerella iliaca*
Rusty song	*Melospiza melodia*
English	*Passer domesticus*
Starling	*Sturnus vulgaris*
Swallow	
Violet-green	*Tachycineta thalassina*
Tree	*Iridoprocne bicolor*
Rough-winged	*Stelgidopteryx ruficollis*
Barn	*Hirundo rustica*
Cliff	*Petrochelidon pyrrhonota*
Swift	
Black	*Cypseloides niger*
Vaux's	*Chaetura vauxi*
Tanager, western	*Piranga ludoviciana*
Tern, Arctic	*Sterna hirundo*
Thrasher, brown	*Toxostoma rufum*
Thrush	
Pacific varied	*Ixoreus naevius*
Hermit	*Hylocichla guttata*
Russet-backed	*Hylocichla ustulata*
Towhee, Oregon	*Pipilo maculatus*
Vireo	
Cassin's	*Vireo solitarius*
Red-eyed	*Vireo olivaceus*
Western warbling	*Vireo gilvus*
Warbler	
Lutescent	*Vermivora celata*
Yellow	*Dendroica betechia*
Myrtle	*Dendroica coronata*
Audubon's	*Dendroica auduboni*
Black-throated gray	*Dendroica nigrescens*
Townsend's	*Dendroica townsendi*
Hermit	*Dendroica occidentalis*

COMMON NAME	SCIENTIFIC NAME
MacGillivray's	*Oporornis tolmiei*
Golden pileolated	*Wilsonia pusilla*
Water ouzel (dipper)	*Cinclus mexicanus*
Waxwing	
Bohemian	*Bombycilla garrula*
Cedar	*Bombycilla cedrorum*
Woodpecker	
Western pileated	*Dryocopus pileatus*
Hairy	*Dendrocopos villosus*
Downy	*Dendrocopos pubescens*
Wren	
Western house	*Troglodytes aedon*
Western winter	*Nannus hiemalis*
Seattle	*Thryomanes bewickii*

Bibliography

ABBOTT, R. TUCKER. *Seashells of North America*. New York: Golden Press, 1968.

BORROR, DONALD J., AND WHITE, RICHARD E. *A Field Guide to the Insects of America, North of Mexico*. Boston: Houghton Mifflin Co., 1970.

BROCKMAN, C. FRANK. *Flora of Mount Rainier National Park*. Washington, D.C.: U.S. Government Printing Office, 1947.

BUCHSBAUM, RALPH. *Animals Without Backbones*. Chicago: University of Chicago Press, 1938.

CLEMENTS, FREDERICK E., AND CLEMENTS, EDITH S. *Rocky Mountain Flowers*. New York: The H. W. Wilson Co., 1928.

COULTER, MERLE C. *The Story of the Plant Kingdom*. Chicago: University of Chicago Press, 1935.

CRAIGHEAD, JOHN, *et al. A Field Guide to Rocky Mountain Wildflowers*. Boston: Houghton Mifflin Co., 1963.

DARLING, LOIS AND LOUIS. *Bird*. Boston: Houghton Mifflin Co., 1962.

FAUBION, NINA LANE. *Some Edible Mushrooms*. Portland, Ore.: Binfords and Mort, 1964.

FURLONG, MARJORIE, AND PILL, VIRGINIA. *Starfish*. Edmonds, Wash.: Ellison Industries, 1970.

GUBERLET, MURIEL. *Animals of the Seashore*. Portland, Ore.: Binfords and Mort, 1949.

————. *Seaweeds at Ebb Tide*. Seattle: University of Washington Press, 1956.

GUNTHER, ERNA. *Ethnobotany of Western Washington*. Seattle: University of Washington Press, 1954.

HALL, HENRY MARION. *A Gathering of Shore Birds*. New York: Bramhall House, 1960.

HASKIN, LESLIE L. *Wild Flowers of the Pacific Coast*. Portland, Ore.: Binfords and Mort, 1934.

HOLLAND, W. J. *The Moth Book*. New York: Dover Publications, 1968.

JEWETT, STANLEY G., et al. *Birds of Washington State*. Seattle: University of Washington Press, 1953.

JOHNSON, MYRTLE, AND SNOOK, HARRY. *Seashore Animals of the Pacific Coast*. New York: Dover Publications, 1967.

KAVALER, LUCY. *Mushrooms, Molds and Miracles*. New York: John Day Co. Inc., 1965.

KITCHIN, E. A. *Distributional Check-list of the Birds of the State of Washington*. Seattle: Pacific Northwest Bird and Mammal Society, 1934.

LEVI, HERBERT W., AND LEVI, LORNA. *Spiders and Their Kin*. New York: Golden Press, 1968.

LYONS, C. P. *Trees, Shrubs and Flowers to Know in Washington*. Vancouver, B.C.: J. M. Dent and Sons (Canada), Ltd., 1956.

McKENNY, MARGARET. *The Savory Wild Mushroom*. Seattle: University of Washington Press, 1962.

MORRIS, PERCY A. *A Field Guide to Shells of the Pacific Coast and Hawaii*. Boston: Houghton Mifflin Co., 1952.

MUNZ, PHILIP A. *Shore Wildflowers of California, Oregon and Washington*. Berkeley: University of California Press, 1964.

MURIE, OLAUS. *A Field Guide to Animal Tracks*. Boston: Houghton Mifflin Co., 1954.

NICHOLSON, B. E., et al. *Oxford Book of Wild Flowers*. London: Oxford University Press, 1960.

PETERSON, ROGER TORY. *A Field Guide to Western Birds*. Boston: Houghton Mifflin Co., 1961.

POOL, RAYMOND J. *Flowers and Flowering Plants*. 2nd ed.; New York: McGraw Hill Book Co., 1941.

RICKETTS, EDWARD F., AND COLVIN, JACK. *Between Pacific Tides*. 3rd ed., revised by Joel W. Hedgpeth. Stanford, Calif.: Stanford University Press, 1962.

ROBBINS, CHANDLER S., *et al*. *Birds of North America*. New York: Golden Press, 1966.

SEYMOUR, E. L. D. *The Wise Garden Encyclopedia*. New York: Grosset and Dunlap, 1970.

SHUTTLEWORTH, FLOYD S., AND HERBERT ZIM. *Non-Flowering Plants*. New York: Golden Press, 1967.

SMITH, ALEXANDER H. *The Mushroom Hunter's Field Guide*. Ann Arbor, Mich.: University of Michigan Press, 1958.

STEFFERUD, ALFRED. *How To Know the Wild Flowers*. New York: New American Library of World Literature, 1950.

STEVENS, WILLIAM CHASE. *Kansas Wild Flowers*. Lawrence, Kan.: University of Kansas Press, 1948.

SUDWORTH, GEORGE B. *Forest Trees of the Pacific Slope*. New York: Dover Publications, 1967.

Index

For the most part this index lists only the common names of flora and fauna. For the scientific names of plants and birds, see lists on pages 231–44.

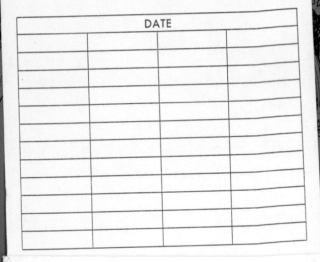

DATE		